THE DANCE ADVANTAGE

RAISING CREATIVE AND
RESILIENT CHILDREN
FOR TOMORROW

Justin Yep & Ineke Vandevyvere

Rethink

First published in Great Britain in 2025 by Rethink Press (www.rethinkpress.com)

© Copyright Ineke Vandevyvere and Justin Yep

All rights reserved. No part of this publication may be reproduced, stored in or introduced into a retrieval system, or transmitted, in any form, or by any means (electronic, mechanical, photocopying, recording or otherwise) without the prior written permission of the publisher.

The right of Ineke Vandevyvere and Justin Yep to be identified as the author of this work has been asserted by them in accordance with the Copyright, Designs and Patents Act 1988.

This book is sold subject to the condition that it shall not, by way of trade or otherwise, be lent, resold, hired out, or otherwise circulated without the publisher's prior consent in any form of binding or cover other than that in which it is published and without a similar condition including this condition being imposed on the subsequent purchaser.

*This book is dedicated to our son
Milan. You are truly a gift.*

We taught him to say, '1, 2, 3, I can do this'.

Now he is telling us to do the same. Ironic.

Contents

Foreword	1
Introduction	3
The transformative power of dance	6
Beyond the dance floor	7
Become the driver	8
The parent's dilemma	9
1 The Age Of Automation	**11**
A Brave New World	11
The AI revolution: Opportunities and challenges	13
The changing landscape of work	15
The digital natives: A new generation	16
Nurturing human skills in the digital age	17
The AI genie: Power and responsibility	19
What remains truly human?	20
Summary: Being human in the digital age	21

2 Dance As Human Expression   **23**
   Is dance universal?   24
   But I can't dance   25
   Dance as communication   27
   Dance brings the world together   31
   The audience's eye   32
   What does dance mean for you today?   35
   Summary: Born to dance   36

3 Can School Solve All?   **37**
   The problems of modern education   38
   Lifelong learning   41
   The shared responsibility for upbringing   44
   The future of hiring   46
   Summary: A new way of learning   48

4 The Classroom Of Creativity   **51**
   Creativity has many faces   52
   The future of creativity and AI   53
   Understanding flow state   55
   The development of creativity across age groups   57
   Overcoming challenges to creativity   62
   Summary: Nurture their creativity   66

5 Resilience — 67
Resilience matters — 68
Cultural perspectives on resilience: Our stories and observations — 69
Our reflections — 70
Barriers to resilience — 72
Building resilience through dance — 73
The superhero — 79
Summary: Preparing for a resilient future — 80

6 The Physical Aspects Of Dance — 83
Dance: A comprehensive body workout — 84
Flexibility in dance — 85
Improved balance and posture — 88
Enhanced coordination — 94
Muscle tone and strength — 96
Neuroplasticity and dance — 97
Kinaesthetic awareness: Your internal compass — 99
The mirror neuron system — 101
Summary: Harder than you think — 102

7 Mental And Emotional Growth — 105
Understanding the 'why?' — 107
Courage: Igniting the spark within (Dream it) — 108

	Completing the process (Do it)	114
	Passing the baton (Give it)	121
	Brain development	124
	Summary: Nurturing the next generation	126
8	**Building Stronger Tribes**	**129**
	The lessons from the pandemic	130
	Building stronger foundations: Hello, thank you, goodbye	131
	Familiarity breeds indifference: The power of multiple voices	132
	Bridging the intergenerational gap	132
	Making real impact: From local to global	133
	Summary: Establish a global mindset in children	137
9	**Hesitations**	**139**
	Boys do dance	140
	Perfect dancing body: A myth	149
	Dance is about expression, strength and joy – not fitting into a box	151
	The risk of injuries	152
	Dance is more than 'just a hobby'	153
	Why dancers make great leaders	154
	Frequently asked dance questions	156
	Summary: Some reassurance	161

10 Dance And The Future   **163**
    From tradition to transformation   166
    The search for balance   167
    The danger and the opportunity   168
    Looking within   170
    Why is it important to find alignment?   171
    Summary: The time is now   173

Notes   **175**

Further Reading   **183**

Acknowledgements   **187**

The Authors   **191**

Foreword

by Jee-Eun Petitqueux

I wish I had *The Dance Advantage* in my hand when I first stepped onto a dance floor. I wish my parents had read it when I was a child. This isn't just another parenting book. As a former professional ballerina, a mum of two boisterous boys, and a dance teacher at the Royal Ballet School in Belgium, I know the benefits of dance and the importance of resilience.

I have faced many challenges throughout my career, on and off the dance floor. My successes and failures have taught me to keep going and to find myself. All of this and more is in this book, which would have been so useful to me in my early days of dance.

What I like is the emphasis on giving children tools for self-discovery. This book shows that children need to have the freedom to explore their desires and create their own identities.

I have known the authors as colleagues in the dance world and as friends. We have watched performances together, had dinner and bowling nights. These experiences have shown me how much they care about children and how creativity builds resilience.

Their approach goes beyond the technical dance and gets to the heart of raising a child. That's what makes *The Dance Advantage* different.

I'm so happy to be part of this book. I love how the authors' knowledge and experience have been distilled into this book. Anyone involved in shaping young minds should read this book. It gives practical tools to raise resilient children and let them be themselves and creative. You will find more than advice in these pages. You will find a way to raise children who, through dance, become beautiful people.

After all, isn't that what parenting is all about?

Jee-Eun Petitqueux
Classical Ballet Teacher at the Royal Ballet School of Antwerp

Introduction

Today's children face a mental health crisis unlike anything we've seen before. As parents, we're caught between wanting to protect them and needing to prepare them for an uncertain future. How do we help them build the resilience, confidence, and joy they'll need to thrive?

We are Justin and Ineke, life partners, co-founders of Ndigo, and proud parents. Our journey began in our twenties, feeling stuck, feeling like misfits and often questioning our place in the world.

Ineke grew up in a small village. It felt stifling. Her ideas often seemed too much for those around her. A teacher once said she was 'too creative' – as if imagination had limits. During an internship at a leading travel agency, she found herself at a crossroads. When they offered her a full-time position, panic struck. Was this what she wanted for the rest of her life? The day after, she found herself at the last possible audition to study dance. She jumped, unsure of the outcome but knowing it had to be something different.

Justin tried everything: coding, selling audio equipment, event management, DJing. But nothing felt right. Job after job, there was always an emptiness he couldn't shake. Then, one day, he was cast in a musical. Something shifted. Dance entered his life at twenty-one – a late start by any standards. It felt reckless, but it also felt like home. At twenty-seven, he decided to study dance overseas. No plan, no roadmap. Just the need to see where this path would lead.

We met at the Fontys Dance Academy. Studying dance did more than give us a career, it unlocked something deep inside. It gave us the courage to face ourselves, to embrace creativity, empathy, and the desire to create something bigger than us.

We had to dig deep. It was about committing ourselves fully, every single day. We woke up early, preparing for ten to twelve hours of classes. We pushed ourselves to question our work constantly: what did we want to express? One thing was certain, it always had to come from a place of honesty and authenticity.

INTRODUCTION

Everyone around us was on the same journey. We felt a true connection with like-minded artists who were also asking those hard, fundamental questions. There was a powerful sense of camaraderie, a shared spirit of growth. No one held back; they weren't afraid to tell us exactly what they thought. It was refreshing, raw and incredibly liberating. It felt like love, a devotion that never once felt like 'work'. When one project ended, we were already excited about the next.

After four years of this, we emerged different people, transformed. We owe so much to the teachers and coaches who pushed us, who believed in us, and who inspired us to dig deeper. It's an opportunity we are endlessly grateful for, a privilege that has shaped who we are today. We consider ourselves incredibly fortunate to have had this experience.

A few weeks before graduating, in Justin's attic room in the student house – the cheapest accommodation we could find, barely covering rent with our student savings – we sat on a bare mattress, no bed frame, and talked about the future. In fact, the majority of the time, we had to sit because the sloping roof on both sides wouldn't let us stand up straight. We didn't have curtains, an old duvet cover hung over the curtain rails did the job. Between study costs, dance equipment costs, and barely making ends meet with weekend work, new curtains weren't exactly a priority. There were mice in the walls because we heard them scampering around at night. But none of that mattered, then. There we were, scribbling dreams into a red diary. We wrote down everything: the career we wanted to build, the kind of lives we imagined, the place we would one day call home. We didn't have answers, just questions and hopes. But we had each other, and we had an idea: to create something meaningful. We wanted to give young people the same chance to feel the way we did – to discover themselves, to find their worth, to feel alive.

Now, we're writing this book. Our dance and yoga studio, Ndigo, is celebrating its fifteenth year. We've received awards, yes, but more importantly, we've received messages – from students, parents, teachers and employees – telling us how their lives have changed for good. These words mean everything. They remind us that dance is so much more than movement. It's a path to self-worth, discipline, and respect.

It is a catalyst for personal growth and empowerment.

The transformative power of dance

Over the past fifteen years, in our studio in Belgium, we've witnessed first-hand the challenges children face: low self-esteem, anxiety and the pressure to conform. But we've also seen the opposite: how dancing can change people. Through this medium, children and teens learn to:

INTRODUCTION

- Change setbacks into wins
- Regulate their emotions effectively, including their anxiety
- Have confidence in themselves and what they do, free from pressures to conform
- Collaborate harmoniously with others
- Appreciate the freedom that comes through discipline

Our philosophy, 'Dream It, Do It, Give It', is a simple yet powerful three-step process that is applicable to all aspects of life. This motto has inspired us and our students to find their place in the world and approach life with confidence and purpose.

Beyond the dance floor

In Belgium, statistics indicate that one in five adults suffers from mental health issues, often traceable to childhood experiences.[1] This book looks at these challenges and provides tools and strategies to help your child thrive in a complex world.

This isn't a book about dance techniques or a sales pitch for classes. We want to tell stories and give advice to help the next generation. We highlight the power of human connection and expression through the art of movement, offering guidance for raising kids in a digital era.

Become the driver

We must be clear: embarking on this journey requires courage. You may face scepticism and pushback, perhaps even from loved ones. You'll be taking a road less travelled, and you'll be challenging conventional wisdom.

We ask you to read this book with an open mind. Many of you have likely encountered naysayers who, out of their fears and limitations, try to discourage new paths with questions like:

- Isn't it a step too far?
- Come on, no one does that, right?
- Do you think you are good enough?
- What is this going to bring you in the future?

The last one is a personal favourite.

These voices of doubt, frequently masquerading as concern, can be powerful deterrents. They represent the status quo, the familiar, and the fear of the unknown. But ask yourself: do you want to navigate your child's future with an outdated map? Are you ready to become the driver of your life – and your child's potential?

The parent's dilemma

As we enter an age of abundance, filled with opportunities and possibilities, many parents find themselves overwhelmed by choice. Do we become helicopter parents, micromanaging all activities and leaving little room for independent growth? Do we become permissive, allowing too much freedom without providing necessary boundaries? We all want our kids to have happy lives that are full of curiosity, creativity, and the ability to handle difficult situations.

The truth lies somewhere in between, and it must be your truth. Your child is unique and deserves a tailored approach to parenting.

Join us on this journey, to move towards a future where your child can confidently declare, 'I am prepared for whatever comes my way.'

1
The Age Of Automation

Imagine trying to explain a smartphone to someone from just thirty years ago. Then picture yourself describing to your grandchildren the world they'll inhabit thirty years from now. The pace of technological advancement is not just rapid, it's exponential, and a new era of Artificial Intelligence (AI) and automation is poised to transform every aspect of our lives.

A Brave New World

We remember the moment this reality truly hit home. Our five-year-old son was video chatting with his Oma, who lives far away. As soon as the call ended, he turned to Alexa and asked her to play his favourite song. It struck us how effortlessly he used these gadgets, which didn't even exist when we were his age. In that instant, we realised how deeply technology is woven into the fabric of our children's lives from the earliest ages.

Today, self-driving cars navigate our streets, virtual reality transports us to fantastical realms, and the sum of human knowledge fits in our pockets. These marvels, once confined to the realm of science fiction, are now our everyday reality. Nevertheless, this is only the beginning. According to recent projections, we're approaching a future inhabited by 100 billion AI agents and a billion robots, a scale that could radically transform our industries, economies and personal lives.[2]

As parents, educators and caregivers, we face a challenge like no other: how do we prepare the next generation for a world where machines increasingly take over tasks once done by humans? Will there be jobs for people in the future? Where do we fit in the picture?

Imagine having a chat with Einstein

THE AGE OF AUTOMATION

The AI revolution: Opportunities and challenges

The human element in many tasks is gradually being supplanted by machines. From self-checkout tills at supermarkets to chatbots handling customer service inquiries, automation is becoming more and more common. Are we being forced out of our world?

It's a concern that strikes a chord not just with adults, but with the younger generation too. Imagine trying to motivate a teenager in school who asks, 'What's the point of this? I'll probably be replaced by software or a machine anyway'. It's a fair question, and one that many of us, regardless of age, are grappling with.

But it's not as simple as tech being good or bad; it's all about how we use it. If young people use technology just to scroll, just to consume mindlessly, they risk losing focus and losing themselves. But when they use it to explore, to learn, to create or to fuel their passions, that's when they thrive. It's like that saying: those who learn to work with technology will be the ones who thrive, while those who ignore it may struggle to keep up.

A 2022 PISA study offers a glimmer of hope: fifteen-year-olds who use digital devices moderately for learning tend to perform better academically and feel a stronger sense of belonging at school.

Conversely, those who spend over an hour daily using technology for entertainment often have lower maths, feel less connected, and are more easily distracted.[3]

This is a story many households know all too well:

> We recently visited some friends, and what we witnessed was all too familiar. Their children were begging for their screens. 'Just five more minutes!' they pleaded, eyes wide with desperation. The parents, clearly tired of this daily battle, reminded them of their ten-minute allowance and handed over the devices.
>
> The transformation was instantaneous. The kids, moments ago bouncing off the furniture, now sat still as statues, thumbs flying over their screens. Then when the timer chimed, signalling the end of screen time, it felt like a switch had been flipped. Content expressions were replaced by scowls of disappointment. The pleas were repeated with renewed intensity.
>
> We watched as the parents' smiles faded. They looked sad and frustrated. It was clear they felt torn, wanting to make their children happy, yet knowing that endless screen time wasn't the answer.

This scene isn't unique. It plays out in homes across the world every day. The solution isn't always clear, and what works for one family might not work for another, but it's a challenge worth tackling head-on.

Here are some tips to help you deal with screen addiction and strike a healthier balance:

- Set an example and limit your own screen time, especially during meals and outings.
- Set a time each evening when all devices are turned off and put away.
- Promote reading, outdoor play, board games or creative projects.
- Keep TVs, computers and mobile devices out of bedrooms to improve sleep quality.
- Engage in physical activities together.

The key takeaway? Balance is the key. Technology can't be avoided, but we parents can set limits and teach our kids how to deal with situations where technology becomes a distraction.

The changing landscape of work

The World Economic Forum's 2020 report paints a picture of dramatic change in the job market.[4] Within five years, they predict 85 million jobs may be displaced due to automation, but they also say that 97 million new jobs will be created that match the changing roles of humans and machines.

This change shows that, as AI and automation take over routine and technical tasks, uniquely human skills will become more valuable. Creativity, empathy, adaptability and complex problem-solving are becoming the new currency in the job market of the future. These are skills that, as of now, no machine, however advanced, can truly replicate.

The digital natives: A new generation

Our personal experiences have shown us just how differently the younger generation interacts with technology. Let us share another example that illustrates this point.

> A few years after the video chat incident described earlier, our eleven-year-old son and his friend were at our house. Instead of complaining about being bored or asking for entertainment, they disappeared into his room.
>
> Hours later, they emerged with big grins on their faces and announced, 'We made a movie!'
>
> And they had! They'd made a proper short film – script, acting, the works.

Shot on an iPad and edited in iMovie, it had transitions and sound effects that would make Christopher Nolan jealous. What's the big deal? They didn't ask for help. Not once.

While we're still trying to figure out which HDMI port to use, these digital natives are making movies in their bedrooms. It's a sobering reminder of how tech-savvy this new generation is and how differently they interact with technology.

Nurturing human skills in the digital age

How do we teach these human skills? You might be surprised with the answer. It's not just about learning to code or using new educational apps. Activities like dance, sports, theatre, music and arts can all help develop these skills.

Take dance, for example. It's more than just exercise or a hobby. Dance taps into human skills like self-expression, creativity and empathy. Children who dance aren't just mimicking moves, they're using their bodies to express feelings and thoughts that go beyond words. Here are some examples:

Imagine an improvisation section, and one dancer has to respond to another dancer's movements or music in real-time. Every so often, they'll lead the dance, initiating a sequence that their partner picks up and transforms. Other times, they'll follow. The key to successful improvisation is staying present. That improvisation will be unique and will never be repeated the same way again.

Next, imagine a challenging lift in a partner dance. Your child is being held high above their partner's head. It looks daring, maybe even a bit dangerous. Here, the dancer being lifted must trust their partner completely, while the supporting dancer must be entirely reliable.

Let's talk about the 360-degree field of awareness. It's like all dancers have a radar strapped onto them that is tracking multiple targets. Children in a group dance learn to be aware of their surroundings and considerate of others. You'll see dancers moving in complex patterns without colliding with each other because they are so aware of the dancers around them.

What about handling the unexpected? When the choreographer has to change whole sections of a dance the night before a premiere because a main dancer is injured, the entire troupe must quickly learn new parts, change places, and support each other.

When we look at the above examples, there is a lot we can learn. Dancers pick up soft skills that are not obvious, but it is these skills that will set them apart and help them thrive, regardless of what the future holds.

The AI genie: Power and responsibility

There's a funny scene in the Disney movie in which Aladdin finds the magic lamp in the cave and meets the super genie (Will Smith). Aladdin asks the genie to make him a prince, to which the genie replies that there is a lot of ambiguity in that request, and that Aladdin must be specific with his words: 'The deal is in the detail,' he says.[5]

As we begin to use AI, we need to understand its nature. Like Aladdin's genie, AI tries to fulfil our desires but needs specific input, a specific prompt. It's a powerful tool, but one that requires careful guidance and clear instructions.

In return, it swallows your data like a black hole. By analysing that data, algorithms get better at predicting what we want. Whether it's Amazon's product recommendations or TikTok's feed, AI is always watching and monitoring us.

With this power comes responsibility. As parents and teachers, we need to teach our kids to use tech to enhance their lives, not replace it. We have to teach them to create and innovate, not just be passive consumers, lost in a digital maze.

What remains truly human?

Using AI the way it's meant to be used is so liberating. We feel so free when AI handles the boring tasks. At our dance school, we're using AI to handle the mundane tasks like programming lighting plans or drafting emails. It handles all our communications, marketing, social media, etc, so we can focus on what truly matters and what we love most – our art, creativity and passion.

But we need to become more human as machines become more efficient. The World Economic Forum lists the key human skills that future employers will look for: critical thinking, leadership, creativity, emotional intelligence and resilience.[6] Throughout this book, we'll explore these skills and how we, as parents, can nurture them in our children to prepare them for the future.

Because these skills can't be developed just through academic achievements. That's why activities like dance are so valuable. Dance is an interdisciplinary activity that combines arts, music, culture, physiology and psychology. It helps us to adapt, evolve and grow agile – all essential skills in today's fast-changing world.

Summary: Being human in the digital age

Our role as parents and teachers has never been more crucial in this new era. We must adapt to technological change, but do so mindfully, with an eye on the long-term impact.

The key to succeeding in the age of automation is not to compete with machines, but to cultivate what makes us human. We're not preparing our kids for the future job market – we're preparing them for a life where human skills are more valuable than ever.

So there you have it. Our humanity is our greatest asset in the age of automation. Let's take care of it in ourselves and the next generation. We do not want to teach them how to just live with machines, but how to exemplify the best of what it means to be human.

2
Dance As Human Expression

You might be wondering why this book is focused on the many advantages of dance, and asking what sets dance apart from other sports or hobbies...

Dance fuses several elements like music, movement and social activity. It has been an integral part of human culture since ancient times, as evidenced in paintings and artefacts from ancient cultures. Cave paintings found in India that are more than 9000 years old show humans socialising and dancing. These cave paintings and carvings are thought to be the earliest proof of dance.[7]

Dance is part of our humanity. It connects the body, mind and soul. It is an instinctive art form that transcends mere words.

Is dance universal?

We frequently observe this phenomenon during our classes with the youngest children. Despite not having learned a single step yet, the three-year-olds joyfully bounce up and down to the rhythm of the music. There is a lot of skipping and jumping, and, obviously, shaking their bums.

Where does this come from?

The ability to move rhythmically comes from a deep connection between music, rhythm and movement. Early in life, children are born with the inherent capacity to detect and respond to pitch and rhythm. It's like they were born with an internal beat, a subconscious understanding that music is meant to be felt with the body.

From a neurological perspective, this instinctual movement can be linked to the way rhythm affects the brain. The cerebellum, the region of the brain responsible for processing rhythm, is already present in young children, and it naturally motivates them to align their movements with their auditory cues. When infants hear music, their bodies respond as if it's second nature. This is the reason that, without comprehending the concept of dance, children engage in rhythmic movement as a means of expression.[8]

Picture this: you are in a bustling bar, surrounded by a lively crowd, the music fills the air, enveloping you and everyone around you. Dozens of people bobbing their heads, tapping their feet with the beat. The act of moving in rhythm feels so innate that we hardly realise we're engaged in a spontaneous dance.

This rhythmic tapping of our feet and the swaying of our heads to music reflect our innate instinct to dance. It is a subconscious connection to the rhythm and melody.

Dance embodies the very essence of being alive, a true expression of life itself. In our studios, we embrace the philosophy that if you can breathe, if you can move, you can dance.

But I can't dance

Why is it as common to hear people say 'I can't dance' when dancing is supposed to be so natural? Some of our friends only dance at parties or weddings, maybe after drinking a few beers. People don't dance because they fear doing it wrong and being judged by everyone, so they avoid it. Some feel intimidated by dancing, as it reveals their emotions and possibly their vulnerabilities. We would like to share a story with you from our wedding party:

Adults of all ages were at the wedding, and we had organised a surprise Bollywood workshop conducted by one of our dancer friends. It was announced that no one could stay seated and everyone had to be present on the dance floor. As you can guess, there were many who had to be pulled from their chairs, frequently followed with nervous laughter and giggles. However, everyone participated.

More than a decade later, many die hard 'I can't dance-rs' still remember vividly how much fun they had on the floor that night. There was laughter, letting go, and a lot of dancing. It had struck an emotional cord, full of bonding between everyone on the floor. Adults from eighteen to eighty given a chance to be free without caring what others thought about them. Maybe that's why the wedding party lasted till six in the morning.

This letting go is most apparent with young children between the ages of three and six who are not concerned with what people think about them. Parents in the studio looking through the window are usually amazed by what they see, and wish they could have had the same freedom as their little ones. Most exclaim, 'Look, they adore dancing, the enthusiasm is so beautiful to watch'. The joy is infectious.

DANCE AS HUMAN EXPRESSION

One of our family beach trips captured this desire to dance perfectly:

> While spending time at the beach, our son's impromptu performance stole the show as we strolled along the shore after dinner. Maybe the feeling of freedom and space on the beach helped him turn it into his personal stage.
>
> He belted out every nursery rhyme he knew, from 'The Wheels on the Bus' to 'Old MacDonald', his voice loud and unrestrained. His dance moves were entirely his own creation, uninhibited and full of vigour. It was mesmerising to watch him, lost in the moment, as if the entire beach was his.

What's most amazing is that we never taught him how to dance like this. Our son's carefree performances remind us how deeply ingrained the desire to dance is.

Dance as communication

Regardless of the form, dance is a powerful means of communication. It can be used to express emotions, tell stories and convey ideas that words can't. Each movement, gesture and step can carry meaning, whether it's intentional or instinctual.

In free-form, improvisational dance, the body becomes an instrument of self-expression. Emotions like joy, sorrow, anger or excitement flow naturally through unprompted movement. Dancers respond to their surroundings, feelings and thoughts, using their bodies to let loose and communicate in the moment. It is a raw and authentic form of communication, and a deeply personal type of dance.

Contrastingly, structured forms of dance, like ballet, folk dance or ballroom dancing, offer a more deliberate form of communication. In these styles, specific movements and sequences tell a story or evoke feelings in a highly organised way. In ballet, for instance, a series of precise movements can tell a narrative without a single word being spoken. Similarly, folk dances often tell cultural stories that are passed down through generations, communicating history, tradition and social values.

Hip hop and commercial dance are modern examples of dance as communication, rooted in expression, individuality and cultural identity. Hip hop gave disadvantaged communities a voice through movement, with breakdancing, popping, locking and freestyle battling becoming powerful forms of self-expression.

Commercial dance, on the other hand, has evolved to meet the demands of popular culture and entertainment industries. Seen in music videos, concerts and television shows, commercial dance blends various styles – hip hop, jazz, contemporary – into performances designed to captivate and engage audiences. It's highly choreographed, energetic and polished, communicating confidence and charisma.

Dancers also communicate with each other in performance. In partner dances, such as salsa or tango, there is a silent dialogue between the partners. They respond to each other's signals, anticipate their movements, and work together to create a conversation through movement.

Music and dance are closely intertwined, but in numerous instances, dancing also creates music. Think of flamenco, tap dance and ancient folklore dances. Dancers incorporated objects that produce sound while moving, such as shells, beads and castanets. They also often stomp and clap, creating body percussion.

Dance inherently invites imitation, as shown by the multitude of young people emulating TikTok dances. Dance, with its emphasis on representation and imitation, may have been an early form of language.

In a study conducted by Steven Brown and Lawrence M Parsons, brain scans of people dancing revealed activation in the area of the brain associated with speech production.[9] The gestures used in dance serve as a means of communication. Imitating movements is important in learning from others and in passing on culture.

Moving together makes a group feel happier and more socially connected. Movement in sync builds:

- Affinity towards each other
- Increased alignment in values
- Prosocial interactions with others
- Heightened trust among participants

Dancing together acts as a social glue. Go into any discotheque to witness this. The DJ sets the beat, and everyone moves to the same rhythm. The group develops movement patterns without instruction. You observe a move, imitate it, and as the DJ lifts their arms, a wave of arms swaying to the music spreads through the crowd. Through the shared music and motion, participants energise one another, communicating nonverbally. It is a state of mind that is similar to a trance. Worries begin to fade as you immerse yourself in the music, freeing your mind from the stress of daily life.

Dance brings the world together

We frequently participate in international dance festivals. At these global events, dancers and choreographers from all over the world come together to showcase their work. Even if we don't speak the same language, their movements often speak directly to our souls. The raw emotions, the storytelling, the sheer artistry – these elements connect deeply with us, proving that dance is a universal language that anyone, from any corner of the globe, can understand and appreciate.

Early humans engaged in dance to connect with something greater than themselves long before writing systems and spoken language existed. Many indigenous cultures have dances as part of their spiritual rituals. For example, the Native American Ghost Dance was performed to reunite the living with the dead and bring about peace and prosperity.

In many societies, dance marks significant milestones in a person's life, such as the Bharaat in Indian weddings – a large procession involving dance and loud music that brings the groom to the bride's home. In agrarian societies, dance often marked the changing seasons and was thought to ensure a fruitful harvest. Examples include the maypole dance in Europe, which welcomed spring and was believed to bring fertility to the land and its people.

Even in the upper classes, dance has been an important form of social interaction, entertainment and even diplomacy. Dances like the French minuet and the English country dance were popular in the seventeenth and eighteenth centuries, allowing the aristocracy to display their refinement, grace and social status. These court dances built relationships, showed one's education and elegance, and often played a role in matchmaking and forming political alliances. For the elite, dance was not merely for pleasure but a structured, symbolic reflection of power, hierarchy and social connections.

So, from the dawn of humanity through to today, dance remains a universal language, crossing cultural, temporal and social boundaries. This universal connection through dance is particularly meaningful for those who may lack the words, the language, or perhaps even the confidence to speak.

The audience's eye

Dance is a two-way street. The audience interprets a performance based on their perceptions and desires, and any dance can hold different meanings for different individuals, with some experiencing a surge of emotions while observing. Many people will feel such an emotional pull when they watch a dance performance. The goosebumps, the lump in the throat, or even an unexpected rush of tears – these visceral reactions are evidence that the dance has touched someone deeply.

DANCE AS HUMAN EXPRESSION

Think of the classical ballet 'Swan Lake'. The story of a swan's impossible love is timeless. Despite its age, the story still resonates by touching on deep human emotions. This classical ballet, with its clear narrative, has captivated audiences for generations, drawing people back time and time again.

What makes 'Swan Lake' truly remarkable is how it offers both comfort and novelty with each viewing. Audiences return, knowing the story and anticipating each act, yet finding solace in reliving this familiar tale. Each performance brings fresh interpretations by artists, nuanced emotions in familiar scenes, and the joy of experiencing Tchaikovsky's iconic score anew. In revisiting 'Swan Lake', people enjoy the artistry and explore their emotions through its enduring themes of love, tragedy and hope.

Modern dance is different because it uses many layers of abstraction. A prime example is the innovative choreographer Merce Cunningham, who fused iPod Shuffle MP3 players with live environmental sounds performed by musicians. Spectators could opt for iPods (provided) or just listen to the ambient soundscape. Imagine the audience united in witnessing the same spectacle, yet each tuned into a different melody. After the show, such unique performances must have led to lively discussions at the bar.

When we saw Crystal Pite's 'Figures in Extinction [1.0]', we could not help but be deeply moved.[10] The choreography, accompanied by recorded sounds of glaciers moving and breaking, was both disturbing and ominous.

As parents watching this powerful piece, we found ourselves contemplating the world our children will inherit. The dancers' bodies transformed into endangered species; their movements capturing both the grace of vanishing wildlife and the violent upheaval of their habitats.

The performance was not comfortable viewing, nor should it be. Each sequence built upon the last, until the weight of our environmental crisis became almost unbearable. This confronting piece compelled us as humans to take action. Today, children are increasingly aware of climate change. Pite's work serves as a reminder that dance, as an art form, can both challenge and inspire society to create positive change.

Contemporary choreographers are always in motion, constantly pushing the boundaries of artistic expression. They are using technology like genome sequencing, motion capture, virtual reality, and artificial intelligence to address complex subjects. They are creating performances that are as intellectually stimulating as they are emotionally powerful.

A dance performance can draw up unexpected emotions in the audience. After a recital, one parent shared with us:

'I still don't really know what exactly happened to me, but I was crying like a little child. My daughter on the stage must have had something to do with it, but the floodgates were open and couldn't be closed any more. The dancer's emotions, choreography, and stage energy struck a chord within me. It revealed new emotions I didn't know I had before.'

What does dance mean for you today?

You should think about how dancing can help your child express emotions, share thoughts and make friends. Typically, the language of children might not be broad enough to properly communicate their emotions, but dance gives them another way of expressing themselves. This can help them grow and learn more about themselves and the world around them.

As their parent, dance offers you a new lens through which to view and understand the complex inner worlds of your growing children.

TIPS FOR PARENTS
- Consider evaluating dance classes to ensure they align with your child's needs.
- Prioritise instructors who cultivate a supportive, nonjudgemental environment, allowing children to freely experience the joys of movement.

- Expose your children to the rich landscape of global dance traditions through online videos, books and local cultural performances.

Summary: Born to dance

Dance is often considered as something of 'low value', or something 'arty'. We discussed in the previous chapter the need to be more human, and dance possesses the unique ability to connect us with our human emotions. It helps us nurture crucial skills such as empathy and emotional intelligence, and beyond just conveying emotions, dance plays a role in helping us process them. By offering a creative outlet for children to express their feelings, dance equips them with the skills to become emotionally resilient and innovative thinkers.

Movement makes you feel better. When you engage in physical activities, like dance, your body releases 'happiness hormones'. It becomes a language, a medium in itself, whether it's about using movement to process emotions or employing dance to communicate and express feelings.

We are just born to dance.

3
Can School Solve All?

School is supposed to prepare our children for life. But in a world that's moving faster than ever, with technology and expectations shifting every day, can we truly rely on schools alone? Are they equipped to keep up, or do we need to rethink how we prepare our children for the future? You may worry:

- That your child is falling behind the others
- That your child isn't being challenged enough
- That your child may not be getting the best education possible
- About mental health and the pressure on your child

While some schools struggle to adapt their curriculum and teaching methods to the modern world, many educators and institutions are actively working to address these issues and innovate in learning.

The problems of modern education

The modern education system was born out of the Industrial Age, when we went from an agrarian society to an industrial one.

Schools were like factories in many ways: mass education, standardised curriculum, administrative hierarchies and strict time management by school bells. Basic skills like literacy and numeracy were needed for an industrialising economy.

This model was designed for an era of factories and mass production and still influences education systems today. Standardised testing, rigid timetables and a focus on compliance are leftovers from that industrial past and clashes with a society driven by creativity and innovation today.

While it's easy to criticise this outdated system, change is complex. We must understand the daily struggles of the school teachers within it. With limited budgets, recruitment problems and extra administrative tasks that teachers have to do, it's no wonder they are struggling. Not lacking will or intention, but many things compound the issue.

CAN SCHOOL SOLVE ALL?

We interviewed several teachers during the process of writing this book. One of them explained to us:

> 'There is not enough time to support each individual. You have twenty students in a class, each with their needs. One student requires extra support, another is on a different learning path, another has challenges. Not everyone speaks and writes the same language. As a teacher, it's very hard to cater to everyone, no matter how much you want to. There is not enough time and teachers to solve this.'

Modern teachers have to juggle:

1. Adapting teaching methods to different learning needs
2. Communication with students, parents and administrators
3. Introducing new tools and platforms to enhance learning
4. Creating engaging and relevant lesson plans
5. Managing classroom behaviour and setting up a positive environment
6. Balancing administrative tasks and teaching responsibilities
7. Doing all this with limited resources

In one classroom, students from diverse backgrounds, with different abilities and learning needs, all come together. This may require extra language support and cultural integration programmes for migrant children, evidence-based interventions for students with ADD or ADHD, sensory-friendly environments for hypersensitive learners and enrichment and acceleration opportunities for highly gifted students.

In Belgium, there are almost 3,200 unfilled positions in the education sector, 20% more than the previous year according to 2023 VDAB (Flemish Service for Employment and Vocational Training) data.[11] This means there is a massive need for more teachers, but the obstacles outlined above may deter people from becoming teachers.

In the past, the teaching profession was highly respected. The teacher in the village was a respected figure and as influential as the doctor or the pastor. That's changing, and many say the profession is undervalued. We must acknowledge the challenges teachers face today and work towards making sure their contribution to society is recognised and supported.

Inadequate technological integration

While technology offers new ways to engage students, its implementation fails due to budget constraints, outdated infrastructure and lack of training for educators.

'One of the biggest challenges is teaching students to use technology responsibly,' explained one teacher we spoke to. 'Developing computational thinking and problem-solving skills is key to this.'

Lifelong learning

Life used to be pretty simple: go to school, find a job, work for forty years, retire, enjoy!

In the industrial age, careers were stable, industries changed at a snail's pace, and if you worked hard, you knew you'd have a pension or savings to rely on. It was a secure, straightforward path—one that promised a comfortable retirement. The modern school system was designed to provide a workforce for the needs of industrialised economies. As factories and large industries became more common, there was a need for workers who were punctual, obedient, and able to do repetitive tasks. The education system was set up to meet the needs of this new economic order.

The school system was based on memorising and retaining information. Success in school meant being able to remember facts and figures, learning structured curriculums, and doing well on tests. This model worked well in an era where knowledge was less accessible and people who could absorb and regurgitate information – whether in law, medicine or business – were highly valued and rewarded with well-paying jobs.

What a drag!

AI and automation are taking over many tasks that used to require human intelligence, so knowing or remembering information is less valuable. The cost of information and intelligence has plummeted as AI can process, analyse and generate data way faster than any human.

As we go through this transition, it takes a human toll. The constant pressure of shifting tasks and pressing deadlines, always being connected and neglecting our physical and mental health leads to breakdown. No wonder many people get burnt out and struggle to stay motivated.

The modern career path is much more dynamic, with people changing jobs every three to five years on average. Around the age of thirty-nine years, many find themselves at a crossroads, contemplating new directions – a midlife moment where it's time to reassess what truly brings us meaning and purpose.

The idea we can absorb all the world's knowledge is simply foolish. Our brains are not built to retain so much information. In fact, the brain tries to get rid of information. Thankfully, today, success is more about ingenuity and resourcefulness, and connecting the dots and continuously acquiring new skills is the norm.

Our journey as business founders is an example of this. Our formal dance training didn't cover major aspects of running a business: sales, marketing, product creation, networking, building sustainable systems or financial management. Once we began, we had to transform ourselves into teachers, bookkeepers, marketing experts, bloggers, psychologists and costume and lighting designers. Oh boy, did we make plenty of mistakes! We couldn't have been more rookie than we were. We didn't start with all this knowledge – we simply adapted and learned as we went along. Google, YouTube and numerous blogs became our teachers. As we write this book, we are also taking an online business course and studying dance pedagogy. Yup, always learning.

This ability to adapt and trust our problem-solving has been the key to our success. The internet has taken learning out of the traditional classroom. Now anyone can learn anything, anytime, anywhere, and at their own speed. Top institutions like Harvard, Yale and MIT offer online courses to people all over the world – whether you're in the UK, India or the Philippines.

'Whatever path you choose, it's not just about learning knowledge; it's also about developing emotional intelligence (EQ),' one teacher told us in an interview. 'By paying attention to EQ in development,' they went on, 'you create individuals who can initiate positive change.'

The top ten skills identified by the World Economic Forum for the year 2023 include analytical and creative thinking, resilience, motivation, self-awareness, curiosity, lifelong learning, technological literacy, empathy, active listening, leadership and social influence.[12] The job market will require a diverse skill set that goes beyond traditional academic knowledge. Knowing where to look is half the battle.

The shared responsibility for upbringing

Children start school at a young age, so a big chunk of 'parenting' responsibility is placed on the education system. Here are some of the things they said:

> 'The responsibility for upbringing is now on the school and the teacher. Some parents think "the school or the teacher" will fix everything.'

CAN SCHOOL SOLVE ALL?

'We can explain to the child why something is important, but ultimately parents have the final responsibility.'

'More and more aspects of upbringing are being placed on the school. Experience has shown me this gets harder and harder every year.'

We know that learning doesn't only happen in the classroom. Some of the most profound lessons come from experiences outside of school, where children can explore and discover the world around them in their own unique way.

Raising our son Milan has been a wonderful learning process for us. He loved playing with toy animals and creating elaborate nature reserves filled with these animals in his playroom. One of our favourite ways to teach him is by going on holiday. His most satisfying trip was going to South Africa, where he saw his favourite animals a few metres away while on safari. He also met other children when he could barely speak English (or so we thought!), and somehow managed a conversation during play. At home, he had never spoken that much English, so we were pleasantly surprised.

However, he also witnessed abject poverty. He saw a man diving for food in a dustbin. The idea that not everyone had a meal to eat struck him hard. There were lessons to be learned along the highway, too. While driving in our air-conditioned car, he observed young children without shoes, walking along dusty highways. One can only imagine they had been walking for hours because we hadn't noticed a village or a rest place along the road.

It opened his eyes and taught him to empathise with different life circumstances, to communicate across language barriers, and to develop a global awareness. It left all of us more thankful for our circumstances. Something Milan would not have got in some textbook.

TIPS FOR PARENTS
- Get your child involved in activities like clubs, volunteering and personal projects.
- Encourage curiosity and adaptation. Travel and explore new places.
- Let your child see change as a chance instead of something to be scared of.

The future of hiring

The job market is changing, with companies like Tesla and Google valuing skills and practical abilities over formal degrees, and future job applicants will need a mix of technical skills, adaptability and strong interpersonal skills.

We wanted to imagine what jobs might be available in the future, so we asked AI to create a job posting as if it was the year 2050. It's likely our children and grandchildren will come across such a listing. Let's play.

JOB POSTING: DIGITAL REALITY DESIGNER (2050)

Future Scape Inc is looking for a creative mind to join our Virtual World Team!

What you'll do:

- *Design cool virtual worlds where people can work, play and live*
- *Fix bugs in our digital universes*
- *Work with AI colleagues to make our virtual worlds fun and safe*
- *Help resolve conflicts between real people and digital characters*

You'll need:

- *Experience with computers and video games (or lots of time spent in parallel universes)*
- *Good imagination and problem-solving skills*
- *Ability to explain complex things simply*
- *Comfortable talking to humans and AIs*

Perks:

- *Work from any reality you choose*
- *Free virtual holiday packages*
- *Time travel insurance (just in case)*

> At Future Scape Inc we welcome all humans, AIs, and everything in between. Apply now by sending a hologram or old-fashioned email. Time travellers, apply before the job is posted.

Summary: A new way of learning

Question: how much of what you learned in school applies to your job today?

Over dinner, Ineke and I pondered this question and we both fondly recalled passionate teachers who made subjects come alive – like my maths teacher, a Christian brother who made equations fascinating (cigarette in hand, no less).

However, we also realised that the skills most crucial to our daily lives and business hadn't been acquired in classrooms, and the real-world challenges we face often require abilities not covered in traditional curriculums. So when parents remark, 'School is most important', our reply is, 'Yes, but…'

This reflection isn't to diminish education's value, but to recognise the importance of lifelong learning beyond the school's walls. It's only one piece of the puzzle. This means that parents are still vital in helping their children learn and grow. Raising well-rounded, educated and resilient individuals is not just the task of schools.

As parents, you need to be involved in your child's learning journey. Trust that when your child is at their extracurricular activities (like dance class), they are working on these skills. If you see the value in alternative education, then you don't need to doubt yourself.

You are doing just fine.

4
The Classroom Of Creativity

When we think about creativity, we usually think about painters, musicians and writers. But creativity goes way beyond the arts – it's about coming up with new ideas to deal with everyday problems. You can use your creativity in many ways, such as:

- Adapting to new technology and preparing for future realities

- Creating an environment that caters to children's different interests

- Making the most of what you have, from budgeting to meal planning

- Finding creative solutions to unexpected difficulties, like work and family life, or meeting the changing needs of children

Creativity is not a fixed trait, but a skill that can be developed over time. We just need to be open and humble enough to learn.

Creativity has many faces

Creativity is needed in many scenarios. See if you can relate to any of the situations that follow, and take note of how many of these skills require creativity:

Your son Darius wants to become a famous YouTuber like Mr Beast. As a one-man operation, he will have to do many things at once:

- Camera work
- Audio
- Lighting
- Video editing
- Graphic design
- Content strategy and posting

Your niece Nina lives in Bali, managing social media accounts for CEOs. She will need to be adept at:

- Persuasive writing
- Research
- Visual design using tools like Canva or Adobe

- SEO and algorithm knowledge
- Network and relationship building
- Self-discipline for remote work

Ron, a cousin, wants to be a dance physiotherapist. He will need:

- Dance skills and knowledge
- A dancer's mindset
- Networking skills
- Content creation skills for platforms like YouTube
- To show leadership in his field
- To partner with other healthcare professionals

As you see, creativity is about seeing the world not just as it is, but as it could be, and then having the courage to bring that vision to life.

The future of creativity and AI

We attended the Flanders AI Forum in June 2024 to bring small and medium-sized businesses a sneak peek into the future of AI. In one of the workshops, each participant received a chart, and we were organised into groups. Each group was asked to brainstorm and imagine use cases where AI could be used to improve their business, and place each improvement under the columns of efficiency, creativity and personalisation.

As suspected, all participants had plenty of ideas for use cases in the column for efficiency. For example, someone mentioned they could feed the transcript of an interview with potential job candidates into AI and see if their values matched those of the company. Another example was using AI to analyse customer feedback from various channels to identify common pain points and trends, allowing businesses to better tailor their products or services. Yes, awesome. As we moved on to the other columns, though, it got tougher to come up with use cases – demonstrating that it is currently difficult to imagine how AI could transform our businesses to become more personalised or creative.

One of the presenters said, 'Look at this audience. Wow! Every seat is full in the auditorium.' It means that business leaders and entrepreneurs are getting ready to use AI in the future. It's inevitable and it's coming fast. This technology is not going in a straight line. It is going faster and faster. Human brains are not designed for exponential thinking, and we frequently misconstrue the rapidity with which things can alter.

If you take thirty steps, you will get across the room. But if you take thirty exponential steps you'll go around the globe twenty-six times. We underestimate the power of exponential growth.[13]

THE CLASSROOM OF CREATIVITY

Take Kodak, for example. They were a giant in the photography world and failed to adapt to the digital revolution. Although they invented the first digital camera in 1975 they were slow to fully adopt it, worried it would kill their film business. Their reluctance to adapt to exponential change led to Kodak filing for bankruptcy in 2012. They were overtaken by the very technology they invented because they didn't think things could change that fast. It's a lesson in how important it is to adapt quickly in a world of rapid technological change.[14]

Many parents have heard of AI and consider it to be a fancy toy or just another trend. But the truth is that there is a gap between what people think about AI and how they actually use it. Only a third of consumers think they are using AI platforms, while actual usage is 77%. Forty-four percent of U.S. adults think they don't regularly interact with AI, which shows a lack of awareness of how deeply AI is already ingrained in our daily technology.

So, if we're heading toward an AI future handling most tasks, our greatest human strength lies in our ability to achieve flow—that state of deep focus and creativity that no machine can replicate.

Understanding flow state

Flow state is a state of intense focus and complete absorption in an activity, resulting in better performance and pleasure. Mihály Csikszentmihályi, a psychologist in the 1970s, coined the term 'flow state' and explained that, when someone's skills match the task they're doing, they feel like they're doing it without thinking about it.

Pieter Mondrian and Leonardo da Vinci also saw a strong connection between art and intuition. Mondrian believed that intuition, which he called the Universal Consciousness, was the source of all true art.[15] Da Vinci thought that art could only be genuine when it was guided by the spirit. He's even believed to have said, 'Where the Spirit does not work with the hand, there is no art'. These artists noticed that the best creative work comes from a deeper place within us.

In his book *Minder moeten, meer FLOW* (translation: *Less must, more FLOW*), Jan Bommerez observes that young children naturally enter flow states during play.[16] Watching young children play with toys, you'll sometimes see this happen, as they lose track of self, time and space, guided by their creativity and intuition.

I believe I can Flow, I believe I can touch the sky

At our camps in Ndigo, children are so absorbed in what they're doing when parents arrive to pick them up, they'll say, 'Oh no, you're here already?' They look disappointed, as if the parent is intruding, interrupting them. It always makes us smile.

This also happens when ten-year-olds have fifteen minutes to make their dance routine and show it to each other. They start making and trying things right away. As the fifteen minutes come to an end, someone always remarks, 'Is the time up already?'

They were in a flow state.

The development of creativity across age groups

Evolution doesn't make any distinction between skills. What we don't use, we lose. The wonder and joy we see in these ten-year-old dancers is because they are fearless and willing to try anything. But we see that the creative flow state doesn't last.

> 'Imagination is more important than knowledge.
> For knowledge is limited. Imagination encircles the world.'[17]
> — Albert Einstein

In Sir Ken Robinson's TED Talk with over twenty-three million views, he says that creativity comes in many forms.[18] We think visually, through sound and kinaesthetically—that is, through movement. Robinson defines creativity as 'the process of having original ideas that have value' and says it should be as important as literacy.

The 1960s Space Race presented NASA with many challenges. During the Cold War, the American space programme had to use new technology and new ways of solving problems to beat the Soviet Union. NASA knew technical expertise and intelligence wouldn't be enough. They required minds that could go in new directions.

NASA asked George Land and Beth Jarman to develop a test to find people with great problem-solving skills.[19] The test was so successful that Land and Jarman used it to study how creativity changes over time. Their study looked at 1,600 children. The results were astonishing.

- At 4–5 years old, 98% of children showed genius level creativity
- By 10 years old this had dropped to 30%
- By 15 years old, only 12% still showed this ability
- And in adulthood, only 2% still had their creative genius

Robinson's observations also match this. He says our educational systems punish mistakes and create a fear of being wrong that kills creativity. Unfettered by this fear, young children show natural creativity.

Traditional education focuses on convergent thinking, which seeks one right answer, not divergent thinking, which seeks many creative possibilities.

He also tells the story of Gillian Lynne, which illustrates this perfectly. In the 1930s she was thought to have a learning disorder (ADHD today) because she was always fidgeting and couldn't concentrate. A considerate doctor realised she wasn't ill. She was a dancer who needed to move to think. Gillian Lynne went on to study at The Royal Ballet School and later choreographed West End shows such as *Cats* and *The Phantom of the Opera*.

Creativity is not a choice. It's a must. The future demands nothing less than a complete reimagining of how we value and cultivate creative thinking in education.[20]

Divergent thinking decreases with age. But why? And what can we do about it?

Let's look at the different stages of development, and see what we can do to help their creativity flourish.[21]

Three to five years

At this stage, children are just beginning to explore movement. Our dance classes for this age group focus on play, imagination and storytelling. Here are some tips for nurturing creativity among this age group:

TIPS FOR PARENTS

- Use creative play with images and stories.
- Encourage their 'I'll do it myself' attitude.
- Set clear boundaries to keep them safe.
- Focus on the fun of it, not on how well they're doing.

Six to ten years

Children at this age are developing their self-awareness and expanding their understanding of the world. To support their creativity:

TIPS FOR PARENTS

- Build cooperation, kindness and being helpful to others.
- Balance screen time with more creative or active play.
- Develop self-regulation.

Here is a simple bedtime ritual that helps our son build connection and skills. We first let him choose a book he loves. A fifteen-minute time limit is set to help him understand boundaries and time management. We then take turns reading, which not only gives him a chance to practise reading itself, but also listening and waiting for his turn. Then we discuss how the character feels, what they do and what happens when they do it. This builds empathy, critical thinking and moral reasoning. The ritual ends by sharing three 'little wins' that brought joy to our day.

Eleven to fourteen years

Adolescents face significant psychological and physical changes and may become more self-conscious. To support their creative development:

TIPS FOR PARENTS

- Keep open and honest communication.
- Teach healthy coping strategies for stress.
- Show them how to replace self-criticism with compassion.

In dance classes, we sometimes start with mindfulness exercises to help students relax and focus, creating a safe space for creativity.

We ask them to close their eyes, take a deep breath and feel the tension in their body. With each exhalation, they release physical and emotional blocks with their breath. This helps them to relax and get into a flow state.

Fifteen to twenty years

Young adults grapple with independence and new responsibilities. Both physical and mental abilities peak, but the pressure to succeed can lead to stress and mental health challenges, making it difficult to maintain a flow state.

TIPS FOR PARENTS

- Give them the freedom to make their own choices.
- Reframe disappointments as opportunities.
- Listen to them, and just be there.

From fantasy play as toddlers, to logical thinking as children, to facing social pressures at school from peers as teens, to making their first adult decisions, life is essentially about solving problems and challenges which become increasingly complex as they develop. That said, when problems start to change, it is a sign of growth.

Overcoming challenges to creativity

Boredom and digital distractions

We both often look back to our childhoods. How we built camps with branches or blankets, and had secret passwords to enter the 'hidden' domains we had created, or played games of cricket when someone brought a bat and ball along. We've noticed a change in the way kids play compared to the past. As kids, we had more free time to invent games, explore and use our imagination. We worry that today's more structured activities, ubiquitous screen time and constant adult supervision may reduce kids' opportunities to be creative and independent.

We understand that parents want their kids to have fun and be safe, but it's also important to let them play freely. There's nothing wrong with letting kids get bored, and sometimes it helps them come up with new things to do.

This is easier said than done, though, of course. It's a Saturday afternoon and you're desperate for a nap, and the kids have been bouncing off the walls all morning. So you give them a tablet, queue up their favourite show and, voilà, instant peace and quiet. You might feel a pang of guilt but, hey, sometimes a parent's gotta do what a parent's gotta do, right?

While it's tempting to use digital devices for instant entertainment, this can inadvertently train children to be passive consumers rather than active creators. Allowing periods of boredom can actually stimulate creativity and independent play.

Binary vs non-binary thinking in creativity and parenting

Justin reflects that moving beyond simple yes-or-no decisions opens up a world of possibilities. As a choreographer, I know that each artistic choice carries countless options. Every gesture and movement holds its own meaning and emotional power.

This approach matters just as much in parenting as it does in art. Life rarely offers clear answers, especially when raising children.

Parents face complex decisions daily. They must balance strict guidance with gentle freedom. These choices are rarely straightforward.

Dr Martin Luther King once said, 'Faith is taking the first step even when you don't see the whole staircase.' We often cannot see where our decisions will lead, but we must still move forward with hope and purpose.

There is beauty in accepting uncertainty. Instead of searching for right or wrong answers, parents can focus on how their choices help their child grow.

Looking back, we often find that our most meaningful paths were not planned in detail. They grew from countless small choices, each made with care and hope. This truth offers comfort to parents who work hard to make wise decisions for their children, knowing that today's choices create tomorrow's opportunities.

Creating a safe space

As dance teachers, we must first create a safe space in which our dancers can open up creatively. Once their armour is cracked open, self-expression starts to feed itself. As they get more confident, they develop their own way of moving. A sense of self emerges, and they can let go of fear and judgement and look within for the answers.

Adaptability

Life is full of surprises. A planned family day out can be ruined by a sick child or sudden rain. True flexibility means accepting these changes without drama. When we parents handle changes calmly, children learn that changes are normal, not scary.

TIPS FOR PARENTS

- Be responsive: Different days require different approaches. Today's tantrum might need a quiet chat, not discipline.
- Stay flexible: Every child is unique. Adapt your expectations to your child's pace.
- Show don't tell: Children learn by watching. When plans change, stay positive. Your calm response helps your child feel safe during changes.

Just as dancers have to adjust their steps to new music or partners, parents have to adapt to their child's changing needs. It's also remembering that flexibility isn't about having no plan. It's about having a plan and being willing to adjust when needed.

Summary: Nurture their creativity

Creativity will be one of the key skills for success in any career in the future. We parents only have a small window in which to nurture this creativity. While it's easy to hand over a tablet or turn on the TV when our kids are 'bored', we need to be creative ourselves. When your child is building with Lego blocks, they might be inclined to a career in architecture or engineering. When they're putting together a magic show for the family, they could one day be a public speaker, TV anchor or even the next David Copperfield. Who knows?

Creativity that is developed, whether through dance, art, or through moments of free play, will last a lifetime.

5
Resilience

Let's start with some words from Ineke about resilience:

'In my first year of the Bachelor Dance Teacher programme in Tilburg, I wasn't selected by the school choreographer for the final performance. Ouch. I felt rejected. My classmates were practising the new piece, but I was left out and felt resentful. I couldn't put my feelings into words, and suddenly I was in a dark place. A few days later, I got to work with a guest choreographer. That helped. I put aside my negative feelings and focused on learning new techniques and perspectives from the new choreographer. I had a great time and felt full of energy again. This experience taught me to see rejection as an opportunity to grow and improve. Feeling down is OK, but it's how you respond that matters.'

Resilience is all about facing challenges like this, changing and coming out stronger. Parents should encourage this in their children, especially given how so many young people are struggling with mental health.

Resilience matters

Recent UNICEF reports show that suicide is the second leading cause of death for young people in Europe between fifteen and nineteen. One in five adolescents in this age group has mental health issues, and nine million adolescents live with mental health issues across Europe.[22] These numbers make it clear how important it is to be strong and resilient. Just like athletes train their muscles, children can train their ability to handle tough situations with confidence and optimism.

How do you think resilience affects your child's ability to handle challenges?

Cultural perspectives on resilience: Our stories and observations

Ineke's story

I grew up in a loving family where honesty, trust, respect, politeness and always doing your best were core principles. This gave me the space to be and become myself. I was often told: 'You can be whatever you want as long as you go for it 100%'.

When I shared my dream of opening a dance studio with my parents, I was encouraged to visualise everything, write it out, put it on paper and pitch it to the family. Without that support, I would never have been resilient enough to take the leap and grab those opportunities. I know I owe that springboard to my family in which I was so lucky to grow up.

Justin's story

My story is more complicated. I was born into a joint Chinese family (three generations living under one roof) that fled the revolution in China and settled in India. I spoke Chinese at the dinner table, English in school, and Hindi on the playground. Preserving the family name came first, so individual success directly contributed to family harmony.

I saw how individualistic selfishness tore my family apart, which I loved so much. That made me more dependent on myself because my idea of family was broken. Since then, my deepest desire has been to get back to that feeling of home and family.

Our reflections

As we raise our child together, it's good to reflect on these different experiences. Our stories show different approaches to resilience, different world views, values and upbringings. Let's explore how these perspectives have shaped our understanding of resilience:

A Western perspective: Individual perseverance and support

Ineke's story shows us aspects of the Western approach to resilience, and how:

- There is a focus on individual potential and dreams

- Family support is about giving individuals the freedom to choose

- There is a proactive approach to visualising and preparing for success

An Asian perspective: Harmony and collective well-being

Justin's background gives us insight into how Asian cultures see resilience through the prism of harmony and collective well-being. In his case:

- 'Eating bitterness' (Chi Ku) was considered a path to growth and resilience
- Family harmony was key, individual success was considered a contribution to the family's pride
- A multilingual upbringing reflects the adaptability required by immigrant families

Even with these cultural differences, we want to give our child a broad and diverse approach to resilience.

Bridging the gap

We understand that every family situation is different, with its own set of experiences, values and challenges. What works for one family won't work for another. What matters is that you stick to your values, where love is the highest aim.

The kind of love[23] that aims to develop and nurture another's spiritual growth but doesn't shield them from all hardships. If you constantly strive to 'protect' loved ones from challenges, you don't allow them to face those challenges. You might think you're doing them a favour by shielding them, but actually you're setting them up for disappointment later on. With the slightest resistance, they may break.

This doesn't mean we have to throw our children in at the deep end without support, but life is a journey of discovery, and sometimes our children must discover things for themselves.

Barriers to resilience

Developing resilience in children can be blocked by many things. An overprotective mother might walk her twelve-year-old to school every day, hampering the development of their children. Social struggles, like a kid eating lunch alone every day because he's shy and doesn't know how to initiate friendships, can impact a child's confidence and ability to build support networks. When parents argue a lot, it can make the home unstable and make it hard for a child to feel emotionally secure. Low self-esteem can make a child more prone to setbacks, like a teenager who stops painting after one negative comment on her work. A lack of positive role models can mean a child doesn't have anyone to learn resilient behaviour from, like parents who consistently avoid difficult conversations and situations. Technology and instant gratification can make children less patient and persevering. They may get frustrated and give up quickly when they can't learn a new dance routine, preferring to scroll through social media instead.

Other things, like fear of failure, academic pressure, bullying, peer pressure and traumatic events, can all add fuel to the fire.

It's often more than one thing. Any one of the above can seriously impact a child's confidence, which can then create a snowball of other problems. Low self-confidence, for example, can attract bullies, leading the child to avoid social situations, and as a result they end up using social media excessively or living in isolated bubbles.

Before you go on, stop and ask yourself if any of these factors affect your child… Write down one small step you can take this week to support them.

Building resilience through dance

Embracing mistakes as learning opportunities

In dance, as in life, mistakes are inevitable. Teach children that errors are stepping stones to improvement. Ineke sits with her ten- to twelve-year-old students, and together they discuss dealing with disappointment like not getting a part in a choreography. In one such conversation, a student wisely said, 'First you cry a little because you're sad, but then you get up, do your best and move on'. It sums up resilience perfectly.

TIPS FOR PARENTS

If your child makes a mistake in dancing or any other activity, use the following steps.

- Step 1: It's OK to be disappointed.
- Step 2: What can we learn from this?
- Step 3: How can we improve next time?

Preparing and visualising

The subconscious brain doesn't know the difference between doing something and thinking about it. Encourage children to prepare thoroughly and visualise success.

For competition dancers this means:

- Arriving early at the venue
- Getting to know the stage
- Practising their routines
- Visualising a successful performance

Spend fifteen minutes with your child visualising success before their next performance. Imagine each step from getting ready to finishing. Make it as multisensory as possible. Visualise the stage, feel the heat from the lights, feel the other dancers preparing for their routine, hear the music from the speakers and feel the emotion of doing it well. This might be applied to anything, from sitting an exam to playing a game of football – make use of the power of the imagination.

Managing physical and emotional responses

Feeling nervous before a performance is completely normal. It's how you respond that matters. Pre-performance jitters can be managed with techniques like breath control and physical warm-ups. Simple yogic breathing can activate the parasympathetic system, calming the body and mind. It regulates the body's oxygen and carbon dioxide levels, which in turn slows the heart rate, reduces stress, and promotes a state of relaxation and focus.

TIP FOR PARENTS

Here's a simple breathing exercise you can do with your child daily:

- Inhale for a count of four
- Hold for a count of seven
- Exhale for a count of eight
- Repeat three to five times

Focusing on impact

Focusing on a fear only magnifies it. Encourage your child to think about how their performance might positively impact others. Our son, when nervous, would focus on this thought before his performance: 'Maybe other boys watching me will get inspired to take up dance despite their doubts'.

Before a challenging situation, ask your child: 'How might your effort inspire or help others?' This question shifts focus from personal fear to positive impact.

Role models

According to Harvard University's Center on the Developing Child, 'The single most common factor for children who develop resilience is at least one stable and committed relationship with a supportive parent, caregiver or other adults'.[24]

While writing this chapter about resilience, we realised once more how important it is for a child to have an adult to look up to, which is something we have observed to be true over the last fifteen years. The dancers we have worked with who were growing up to become strong personalities always had a visible and positive adult in the background. Such adults would help plan, advise and be their biggest cheerleader.

Discuss role models with your child. These could be dance teachers, family members, or any other trusted adult. Can you identify someone who may fit the role for your child?

Peer support and motivation

Dance classes with the right values create a unique space for peer learning and support. In those spaces dancers can see how their peers tackle tough movements or routines, they can celebrate together and learn to deal with emotions in a group. A group of friends who get it makes everything better.

In our dance teams, role modelling and peer support is at the heart of growth. Younger dancers look up to the older ones, even if they're just a year or two older. It's amazing how much perspective a younger dancer can get from someone just a step ahead of them. And for the older dancers, teaching and guiding their peers helps them reinforce their own skills and understanding. It becomes a beautiful cycle—everyone learning, everyone growing and everyone pushing each other to be better.

Get your child to set up a 'buddy' with a peer. They can check in with each other, support each other and celebrate each other's progress. In Chapter 7 we will go into more detail about the buddy system. Peer support helps children overcome anxiety and stage fright by offering encouragement, companionship and confidence. Let's read about Nanne and Oskar.

The story of Nanne and Oskar

Nanne, a seven-year-old dancer, was overcome with stage fright. It was terrifying for her to be in front of an audience. She froze at first and didn't move. Hesitantly, she set about moving along with the rest of the group. Fast-forward, and Nanne became more confident as the shows went by, and during one particular camp, the teachers noticed a change in Nanne's mindset. She seemed eager to perform. In the same camp, another shy three-year-old boy, Oskar, was about to go into his first performance. He was also nervous. He was so frightened he covered his face with his hands and didn't want to step onto the dance floor. Noticing this, Nanne walked over and took Oskar's hand and whispered that everything would be OK (during the showcase for the parents).

The audience watched on, astonished. No one had asked her to do that. Yet she did. She saw herself in Oskar, and she was going to do something about it.

They performed together that day and left the stage hand-in-hand, with the audience cheering loudly. Nanne and Oskar's parents were touched and tears flowed. Everyone saw that something beautiful had transpired. Something kind. Something mature. Nanne not only showed resilience and conquered her fears, she also empowered Oskar to do the same.

The superhero

What if you could boost your confidence just by standing like your favourite superhero? Have you ever noticed how superheroes stand—feet planted firmly, shoulders back, head held high? It's no coincidence that this powerful stance makes them look unstoppable.

Studies strongly suggest that physical activity and improving posture can change brain networks to improve mental skills and help people to handle stress better.[25] Dance training is particularly appealing because of its focus on posture and alignment.

Tony Robbins, a coach, talks about how physical posture can affect our mental state.[26] A Harvard study later backed up his idea.[27] Just standing in a powerful pose like your favourite superhero for two minutes can make you feel confident and willing to try new things.

The foundation of posture is hammered into dancers from the beginning. Posture is the ability to stand tall, to project confidence and counter the effects of gravity. When a person enters a room radiating self-assurance, just notice their posture. On the other hand, if one would imagine a person with the life sucked out of them, what posture would come to mind?

We'll get into the physical benefits of dancing in the next chapter.

Summary: Preparing for a resilient future

Life is a journey along an uncertain path. As parents, we want to give our children a sense of self-reliance that will help them survive and succeed in life. Imagine your child walking along a path and finding a massive boulder in their way. The boulder could be a career setback, a health challenge or a global crisis. The specific obstacle isn't what matters. What matters is the determination to overcome it, the creativity to find a solution, and the stamina to push through.

This is the essence of resilience – to last no matter what. It's about developing that inner strength, that quiet resolve that whispers 'I can, and I will', even when the odds are impossible. Whether your child chooses to climb over the boulder, go around or tunnel under it, the key is they don't get defeated and keep pushing towards a solution.

Resilience isn't just about individual survival. The true measure of resilience is how we use our strength to lift others, to contribute to society, and to tackle the big challenges of the world. We're raising children who see every challenge as an opportunity to raise the bar, not just for themselves, but for all.

RESILIENCE

Through dance, we give our children a microcosm of life's journey. Each routine is a path, each mistake a boulder to overcome, each hesitation is a fork in the road. We parents provide the steady hand in the background, encouraging, supporting, but letting them find their own path.

6
The Physical Aspects Of Dance

'The spirit is willing, but the flesh is weak.' This age-old principle reminds us that, to achieve the highest possible evolution of the human spirit, we must first train and prepare the body.

Throughout history, cultures have recognised the connection between physical preparation and higher spiritual pursuits. Indian yogis and sadhus used asanas (postures) and pranayama (breath control) to deepen meditation and maintain focus. Similarly, Shaolin monks of China developed martial arts for self-defence, combining rigorous training with moving meditation for a holistic spiritual practice.

In this chapter, we make our case for dance as the ideal physical activity to nurture resilient and fit children who are ready to face the challenges of the future, and we'll look at how dance builds strength, flexibility, coordination and endurance like few other activities.

Dance is a perfect blend of art and athleticism that can be turned from a fun hobby to a physically demanding profession. Our journey as dancers, dance educators and parents of a child who loves to dance, has granted us a unique perspective on the physical demands and benefits of dance. We believe in a simple trinity: move well, eat well, sleep well.

It can be hard for parents to choose the right physical activity for their kids. There are many options, each with its advantages. Dance as a hobby is undoubtedly fun and a great way to learn new skills. But at its most intense, professional dance is one of the most demanding physical activities one can pursue. Dance can give your child the right level of physical challenge and growth. A child's dance journey can be time-consuming. For parents, it means being a personal chauffeur, juggling schedules and making sacrifices. But we can assure you, the rewards – seeing your child grow stronger, more confident, and more resilient – are absolutely worth it.

Dance: A comprehensive body workout

Dance engages the entire body, offering a uniquely holistic exercise experience. Unlike sports that target specific muscle groups, dance improves overall physical health and stamina; enhances coordination, balance and flexibility; and challenges diverse muscle groups through varied movements.

This diversity prevents physical plateaus by continuously introducing new challenges. Training that is age-appropriate keeps the muscles in balance and avoids muscle imbalances that are common in sports.

Dancers can develop a comprehensive, functional fitness that improves both performance and everyday movement.

Flexibility in dance

This section is not a comprehensive guide on improving flexibility. Rather, we aim to discuss flexibility's role in dance, recognising its deeply personal nature.

Flexibility training is a cornerstone of dance, enabling graceful and fluid movements, maximising range of motion and preventing injuries.

The reality of flexibility

Young dancers scrolling through TikTok or Instagram Reels may feel discouraged when comparing themselves to ultra-flexible influencers. However, it's absolutely essential to understand that extreme flexibility doesn't determine one's ability to dance. We advocate for a patient, gradual approach, especially with young children.

Flexibility improves over time with consistent practice and patience. It's important to focus on enhancing the range of movement, as flexibility depends on the interplay of bones, muscles, tendons and ligaments surrounding the joints.

Michelle's story of success demonstrates this nicely.[*] Michelle was a ten-year-old student who set herself a goal to achieve full splits on both sides during her summer break. She began by photographing her initial pose. Each day, she diligently practised the exercises learned in class. After eight weeks of consistent effort, Michelle proudly shared a new photo with us. Her progress was remarkable – she beamed as she successfully performed the splits on both sides.

Types of stretches

There are several stretching techniques that dancers can employ:[28]

- Static – Passive stretches where muscles are not engaged
- Static – Active stretches have muscles engaged and loaded

---

[*] Names throughout the book have been changed to maintain anonymity.

- Dynamic stretches involve continuous movement throughout range of motion
- Proprioceptive Neuromuscular Facilitation (PNF) uses the stretch-contract-relax-stretch-repeat process.

For dancers, it's crucial to implement a balanced mix of these techniques. The focus should be on gradual progression, respecting each individual's capabilities. These stretches are performed regularly during the week at 30-40% intensity, for thirty seconds per pose.

Safety considerations

Stretching should be conducted when the body is warmed up, typically during or at the end of class. It's essential to maintain a steady pace and to never force stretches through pain.

Stretch tolerance – an individual's capacity to endure stretching discomfort – varies based on factors like age, sex and dance background. Dancers must recognise their body's limits and take responsibility for their training. Understanding the difference between 'good pain' (the beneficial discomfort of stretching) and 'bad pain' (signalling potential injury) is vital. We educate our dancers to distinguish between these sensations to ensure safe practice.

Flexibility training requires striking a delicate balance. While we aim to achieve an optimal range of motion, our primary concern is always the safety and well-being of young dancers.

Improved balance and posture

In Chapter 5, we touched upon the importance of posture in building resilience. Now, let's delve deeper into the physical aspects of posture and its significance in dance.

Defining posture and balance

Posture is how we hold our bodies while standing, sitting or moving. Good posture is the alignment of body parts supported by the right amount of muscle tension against gravity. Balance, on the other hand, is our ability to distribute our weight to maintain stability while stationary or in motion.

Together, posture and balance are crucial, not just for dancers, but for everyone. They influence how we perform daily activities and maintain overall health.

The stand-out effect

Good posture doesn't come naturally to most people. In our classes, it's one of the first things we teach – how to stand correctly. During our American Ballet Theater teacher training, we learned about children's postural development and we made a number of observations about how children's posture develops at different ages. Children between three and seven years tend to show the following traits:

- They often stick out their tummies.
- Their pelvis tilts forward, creating a hollow back.
- The upper back and head compensate by pulling backward.
- Feet are usually pronated, with arches falling inward.

We gently bring these issues to our young dancers' attention, using imagery and mimicry to help them correct their posture.

As they grow into teenagers, we notice a striking contrast, and that non-dancing teens tend to slouch, with their shoulders drooping, their heads forward and their backs rounded. This is the opposite of what we see in three- to seven-year-olds.

Have you ever noticed someone in the crowd who just seems to stand out effortlessly? Could it be their posture or the way they move? Imagine if your child could develop that kind of confidence and presence through dance.

The role of dance in improving posture

Dance offers a unique and effective way to enhance posture and balance. Let's look at how.

Core strength: By performing movements like lifts and controlled extensions, dance training actively engages the core muscles – abdominals and back – creating a strong foundation for good posture.

Alignment awareness: Through precise positioning, such as keeping the spine straight during a ballet plié, dancers develop constant awareness of proper body alignment.

Weight distribution: Dance teaches proper weight distribution, in shifting weight smoothly from one foot to the other, like in a waltz, which is crucial for balance.

Consistent practice: Regular dance training, such as weekly training of posture-focused exercises, reinforces good posture habits.

While some individuals may have a natural advantage in balance due to genetics or lifestyle, anyone can improve through targeted exercises and consistent practice.

Standing tall

Alice, a sixteen-year-old dancer at our studio, is a great example of how dance can change posture and self-esteem. After her parents got divorced, Alice found comfort in dancing. She would slouch with hunched shoulders, as if she wanted to go unnoticed. Alice slouched so much that a doctor suggested physiotherapy, but she had trouble doing the exercises at home.

The physiotherapy didn't help, but ballet did. It provided Alice not just with an outlet for her energy, but a new way to engage with her body. Over time, the impact of dance on Alice's life became obvious. Her posture improved significantly, both in and out of class. She began to stand taller, with her shoulders back, radiating a newfound confidence.

As her mum noted, 'Alice is much more comfortable in her skin now. She no longer fades into the background among her friends. She is beginning to embrace her true self after going to ballet. She always comes back calmer and joyful.'

Self-esteem linked to posture

A study published by *Health Psychology* offers compelling evidence for how posture directly influences not just our physical state, but also our psychological well-being.[29] The study involved seventy-four participants in New Zealand, who were assigned either a slumped or straightened posture. This posture was maintained using tape, ensuring the consistency of the experiment. Researchers then monitored their blood pressure and heart rates while engaging them in tasks designed to assess mood, self-esteem and stress levels.

The results of this study resonate strongly with what is taught in dance classes worldwide. Participants who maintained an upright posture reported feeling more energetic, enthusiastic and stronger. Conversely, those in a slumped posture experienced feelings of fear, hostility, nervousness and a general sense of sluggishness.

Interestingly, the study went beyond just physical health metrics. Participants with good posture also exhibited higher self-esteem, less social fear and fewer negative emotions. Additionally, they demonstrated stronger pulse responses compared to those with poor posture.

Modern challenges to good posture

These days, maintaining a healthy posture has become increasingly challenging for our children. With little physical activity, they're often hunched over smartphones, tablets or computers, leading to a forward head posture and rounded shoulders. With so much time spent sitting – whether at school or playing video games at home – their core muscles can weaken, causing them to slouch more. Remember those heavy backpacks we used to carry?

Well, they're still a thing, and lugging around all those books strains their backs and shoulders. If a child is dealing with extra weight, it adds more stress to their spine and muscles. Plus, when they hit those growth spurts, rapid changes in their bodies can throw off their alignment.

'Rising screen time is causing a rise in back pain among kids and teens,' noted Erika Barger, a physical therapist at the UC Health SportsMed Pediatric Therapy Clinic in Steamboat Springs.[30] As young people spend a lot of time on their devices, they lose their natural posture and balance.

TIPS FOR PARENTS

Take a moment to check your posture now, while you're reading this. Here are some ways to improve your posture, whether you dance or not:

- Regular physical activity, especially dance.
- Focus on exercises that target abdominal and back muscles.
- Practise the 'Superhero Pose' described at the end of Chapter Five: stand with legs apart, back straight, hands on hips, and chin slightly lifted. This 'power pose' can boost confidence and improve posture.

- If sitting for long periods, take regular breaks to stretch and move around.
- Pay attention to your posture throughout the day and make changes if needed.

Enhanced coordination

Once your child has developed good posture and balance, the next key step is coordination. With good coordination, movements become smoother and more efficient, helping to reduce effort and any sense of awkwardness.

Coordination is the art of using different parts of the body together in a smooth, efficient manner. Dance involves complex movements that require precise timing and coordination between different parts of the body. This improves both fine and gross motor skills.

Imagine a ballet dancer executing rapid, intricate footwork while their arms move gracefully. Despite differing speeds, upper and lower body movements are seamlessly integrated, demonstrating a high level of coordination.

Improved coordination leads to smoother, more enjoyable movements. It lowers joint strain and reduces injury chances. For example, a dancer landing after a jump knows how to plié (bending knees) to protect their joints.

THE PHYSICAL ASPECTS OF DANCE

Anais' story demonstrates this nicely.

Anais is a dancer, who we first met when she was five years old. She looked like any healthy and normal girl you would know, but there was an issue.

Anais was born with problems with one of her hands that needed surgery as soon as she was born. She had difficulty with her fine motor skills as she grew up. Her mum noticed that Anais was reluctant to use her 'weaker' hand and asked us to help her.

In our weekly classes, we practise hand-eye coordination and finger strength with fun tasks. The dancers 'pluck flowers from the sky' or 'play piano' on the floor, gently encouraging fine motor control.

This resulted in improved hand-eye coordination. As her fingers got more dexterous, she also developed more strength in her affected hand. Her parents and doctors also noticed that she was now more coordinated. The very fact that she had got this far was remarkable, according to her doctor. He instructed Anais to keep dancing.

While Anais may not be as dexterous as others, she finds joy and self-assurance when she dances.

Muscle tone and strength

Unlike the isolated muscle exercises you might see at a gym, dance promotes full-body strength. Jumps build leg power, lifts use upper-body strength, and sustained poses develop core stability. Above all, dancers must maintain control over every muscle and mask the intense physical effort. They have to make it look easy, while making it look 'easy' is anything but easy.

The invisible strength of dancers

Dance teachers all over the world give this example to beginning dancers. When you see a beautiful swan travelling over water, you see a lovely bird. Above water, the swan looks effortless and calm. Under the water, though, she's furiously paddling, something we never see.

Now imagine your child effortlessly executing a series of pirouettes or skilfully lifting a dance partner. The strength required for these feats is immense, yet it's often invisible to the audience. This is where dance differs from traditional sports:

- **Sustained power:** While a sprinter's strength is seen in a brief burst, a dancer maintains strength throughout an entire performance, sometimes for hours.

- **Flexibility meets strength:** Dancers develop the unique ability to be both strong and flexible. This balance allows them to hold difficult poses and move with incredible control.

- **Lean and powerful:** Dance builds strength without bulk. The focus is on strong, lean muscles that allow for a wide range of motion and artistic expression.

Neuroplasticity and dance

Remember when your child first tried to tie their shoelaces? It seemed impossible at first, with fingers fumbling and laces tangling, but after days of practice, suddenly it clicked. This same process happens when a child starts dance classes. At first, their body might not cooperate, but with time, those awkward movements transform into controlled steps. What's happening here isn't only physical learning – something called neuroplasticity is also at work.

Neuroplasticity, in simple terms, is your brain's ability to change and adapt as a result of experience. Imagine your brain as a jungle, filled with pathways. Some of these pathways are well-trodden, easy to walk through because you use them a lot. These are your existing skills and knowledge. But when you start learning something new, it's like hacking a new path through the jungle. At first, it's tough and slow-going, but the more you walk that path, the easier and more automatic it becomes. That's your brain creating new connections and strengthening them each time you practise.

When you learn, your brain cells (neurons) communicate with each other through synapses (connectors). Every time you repeat a task or think about a new concept, this strengthens the connection between those neurons.

Regular dance practice helps children develop stronger neural pathways, improving their overall learning ability. And learning different choreographies in different styles further enhances the brain's memory, control and creative centres.

The long-term benefits of dance

A study was done by the European Federation of Neuro Rehabilitation Society.[31] Healthy seniors and individuals with mild cognitive impairments such as Parkinson's were observed to benefit from dance. Dance evoked joy, and that positively promoted brain plasticity. Dance sessions over several months caused structural brain changes, as shown by brain scans, especially in areas related to motor control, auditory processing, language skills and memory retention.

These findings suggest that dance may have the potential to support brain health across all age groups. If dance can help people where neuroplasticity is compromised, it makes sense that its effects on younger, more adaptable brains could be even more profound.

Kinaesthetic awareness: Your internal compass

Imagine dancing blindfolded in a room full of people, relying solely on your sense of touch and internal awareness of your body's position. This isn't a hypothetical scenario – it's a real experience from Justin's dance career, as he explains:

> 'I was employed by a choreographer who was creating a blindfolded duet between me and another dancer. We first learned the routine without blindfolds until we knew it inside out. Then came the moment of truth: dancing it blindfolded. Surprisingly, we didn't crash into each other. The real challenge was performing this in a 15x10m room with the audience present and spread out on the dance floor. We had to adjust to this new dimension, relying entirely on our sense of touch, hearing and proprioception while the audience were around us.'

This performance shows how kinaesthetic awareness can be used to know exactly where each body part is and how it's moving.

How can we develop this? We use simple exercises and techniques in our dance classes to increase kinaesthetic awareness:

- **Closing eyes:** Practise balancing on one foot with the eyes closed. This forces a child to rely on their body's internal sense of position instead of visual cues, improving their kinaesthetic sense.

- **Slow motion:** Walking in slow motion. This helps a child become more aware of each phase of the movement and how their body feels.

- **Mirrorless dancing:** We often dance away from the mirror. Mirrors can make it hard for a child to feel movement inside. Dancing without visual feedback encourages a child to trust their body's sense of space and movement.

- **Body scan:** This involves lying down quietly and mentally scanning the body from head to toe. This mindfulness exercise increases awareness of tension and relaxation.

- **Other exercises:** Using tools like balance boards or bosu balls (uneven surfaces) in training sessions can also help a child's balance and proprioception.

Dance helps children move with agility on the playground, cross a busy street, and make quick adjustments to avoid obstacles. By developing kinaesthetic awareness, a person becomes more aware, coordinated and safe.

The mirror neuron system

Imagine your child watching a performance, where they feel like they are moving with the performer. This connection they feel with the dancers has a lot to do with something in the brain called the mirror neuron system. These special neurons fire up when we do something ourselves or, importantly, when we watch someone else do something.[32]

This system plays a big role in how we learn to dance:

- **Watching and doing:** Because these neurons help the brain simulate the action, they make it easier for a child to imitate what they've seen. That's why they might pick up a new dance move after watching it only once, even if they've never tried it before.

- **Emotional connection:** This is what sells live performances. An outstanding stage performance can make the audience feel every emotion. We humans want to feel struggle, pain, deceit or joy during a performance.

- **Accelerated learning:** The brain is constantly absorbing and processing new movement patterns, even when the dancer isn't physically practising. That is why, worldwide, injured dancers are always invited to watch a class or a rehearsal so that they remain part of the process, and can pick up once they are back on the dance floor.

In simple terms, the mirror neuron system is the reason we learn more effectively when we see someone demonstrate a task or action.

Summary: Harder than you think

Each year we hold a ballet examination to test the abilities of our students. The parents are invited to be part of the examination, so they also understand the effort dancers put into their hobby. At the end of the examination, we often hear, 'That looked really hard', or, 'Wow, I didn't know that required so much effort'.

You know what it is? Traditionally, the audience were not participants in performance preparations, and they were only shown the 'final result'. However, we noticed that parents became much more involved once they observed the rehearsals and the preparations. Because dancers are trained to make their movements look effortless, many people don't realise just how physically demanding dance truly is. It's easy to overlook the fact that dance requires effort just as sports like rugby, or even labour intensive activities like construction work. Dance may appear graceful and effortless, but it demands immense strength, endurance and resilience.

Researchers at InsuranceProviders.com used data from the Occupational Information Network (O*NET) and found that a professional dancer ranks higher in physical demand than jobs like construction or professional sports.[33] You heard that correctly – dance is harder than you think.

Now that you understand all the physical benefits of dance, the next step is to apply it. The true power of dance comes alive when you move.

> 'Knowing is not enough, we must apply. Willing is not enough, we must do.'[34]
> – Johann Wolfgang von Goethe

7
Mental And Emotional Growth

Let's start with the story of the bamboo. A farmer planted some seeds and tended them daily. He watered, fertilised and cared for them without fail, and yet after several years passed, there was nothing to show for his efforts.

The farmer still continued.

One day, a tiny shoot appeared. Within weeks, it grew explosively, seemingly like magic. Each day, the bamboo plant grew higher and higher, and thicker and stronger.

The bamboo plant had bided its time. All those years, it had been busy developing an intricate root system underground, unseen under the soil.

The metaphor of the bamboo in this story reminds us about raising children. Children require plenty of nurturing, guidance and attention before their young minds begin to show the results of all the efforts their parents put in. It's only much later that parents and everyone around them notice the changes and, during a proud moment, they utter the same universal words: 'Look at how they've grown... where has the time gone?'

All parents want their children to find purpose and have the best possible chance to develop into a full human being. They would also want their offspring to be able to surround themselves with solid, nurturing relationships. Humans are social beings, after all. The ability to convince groups of people at a time and rally them around a common vision will determine the speed and the success of many human endeavours.

At the core of this lies a deep-seated desire for our children to grow up with *emotional intelligence*, not just to manage one's own feelings, but also to understand the feelings of others. The quality and depth of human relationships play a critical role when we talk about fulfilment and happiness.

Parents and teachers need to be able to keep working like the bamboo farmer, putting in the time and effort with their daily actions. And like the farmer's seeds, dealing with emotions is never straightforward – it's quite simply a lot of work.

There are many paths to the same goal. Our view of success has shifted according to the times. Maybe growing older has something to do with this, but looking back, we both chose a path less trodden. Aristotle's definition of a successful life hangs around the concept of eudaemonia, which translates to flourishing or well-being. Similarly, the Japanese term 'ikigai' represents finding purpose and meaning in life, which aligns closely with the idea of achieving well-being and fulfilment.

Success is not solely measured by external achievements like wealth or fame, but by the inward development of one's character and the realisation of a person's full human potential.

Understanding the 'why?'

Understanding the 'why' behind our actions and desires acts as a compass, guiding us through life. When we narrow down what truly brings us happiness and inspiration, the paths to achieve the 'what' and the 'how' naturally unfold before us. However, this process is not simply a test of our intellect in solving problems, it demands that we look inward, into the corners deep inside. We must be prepared for questions or answers we may not want, and understand that ignoring or postponing them won't make them disappear—they could be the very things holding us back.

In this chapter, we would like to show how dance stimulates and enhances your child's emotional intelligence. Over the fifteen years we've had Ndigo, and over which we have taught thousands of students, we have noticed the challenges that keep repeating. We have had to struggle to distil it down to a simple process to explain what, we believe, is an excellent formula for creating dancers that are hyperaligned and truthful to themselves.

You've already seen our motto in this book earlier – Dream it, Do it, Give it. It is not simply marketing speak, but a simple framework we follow that injects all the required elements to achieve our goals.

Courage: Igniting the spark within (Dream it)

At Ndigo, we firmly believe that courage is the first step towards manifesting dreams into reality. This bravery forms the first steps of a child's journey. It starts with the individual. We sit down and put forward some simple questions. Nothing too complicated. The goal is to be able to open up the student so that he or she is receptive to expressing.

MENTAL AND EMOTIONAL GROWTH

Students are encouraged to put their thoughts on paper. This could be in the form on writing down words on paper, or some prefer to draw or sketch in a journal.

This process helps dancers to understand the 'why' (their deepest desires) behind each aspect of their dance education, creating a sense of purpose and meaning in their journey. It also encourages them to think with a growth mindset.

Growth vs fixed mindset

To help children grow mentally and emotionally, it's important they have an open mind, rather than a fixed mindset. Our goal is to help shift their mindset from a rigid self-view to one that embraces flexibility, openness and growth.

A growth mindset means believing in the potential for change and development, unlike a fixed mindset, which sees these traits as unchangeable. This mindset transforms 'I can't do that' into 'I can't do this yet, but I'm learning'. It turns the thought 'This workshop is too difficult' into 'This workshop is challenging, but it's an opportunity to grow'. And it changes 'Everyone else is better than me' into 'Everyone grows at their own pace, and I will focus on my journey'. This is a process of reframing thoughts and beliefs into something much more gentle and fluid.

This process is not limited to the dancers. Even the parents should be mindful of the words and beliefs they project. Expressions like 'I'm not good with computers' or 'I can't do languages' model a fixed mindset to children, limiting their belief in their own potential.

Instead, showing openness to learning and growth can inspire them.

When faced with setbacks, or when peers seem to advance more quickly, it's easy to hit a metaphorical wall, but like soldiers learning to scale an obstacle wall in training, setting mini-goals helps dancers to overcome these barriers. We encourage them to set personal challenges, capturing their starting point with a photo or video, then observing their progress over several weeks. This before-after practice has led to remarkable achievements dismantling self-imposed limitations.

MENTAL AND EMOTIONAL GROWTH

In essence, the labels we assign ourselves or accept from others are not definitive truths.

In the Ndigo 'buddy system', every dancer is paired with a 'buddy' – a fellow dancer who becomes a source of support and motivation. The idea is simple yet powerful: each dancer shares their personal goal with their buddy. Together, they break this goal down into smaller, achievable steps that can be worked on week by week.

At the start of each dance class, buddies check in with one another, tracking progress and celebrating each step forward. Whether it's mastering a tricky technique, building strength, or growing in confidence, the buddy system fosters accountability and encouragement.

For non-dancers, think of it like a sparring partner in boxing, a study partner in school, an accountability partner in business or a workout buddy at the gym; someone who keeps you on track and pushes you forward. It creates a positive cycle of mutual support where dancers cheer each other on, keeping each other motivated to reach their goals.

Allowing for failure

'Embarrassment is the cost of entry. If you aren't willing to look like a foolish beginner, you'll never become a graceful master.'[35]
— Ed Latimore, Boxer

Dance poses its challenges, but so does life. It's crucial for your child to understand that making mistakes is not only normal, but necessary. When your child starts something new, for example dancing, they are indeed beginners. Then, it feels like their limbs are going in all directions except the one they want. But then they get the hang of it, and unexpectedly perhaps, it starts to work. As their journey improves, their self-confidence can only grow as a result.

Such an environment is a great catalyst for students who have not dealt with failure often. For high achievers, the dance floor becomes a space where effort, not just effortless success, defines growth. It teaches the invaluable lesson of a growth mindset, preparing them for a future that values adaptability and perseverance.

Recently, we heard a lovely story from a mother. She has two daughters, the older one is in her early twenties, and the younger one is twelve years old. Her oldest daughter did not pursue dance or a similar hobby.

She is quite a perfectionist and has excelled academically, achieving high scores and success. However, she struggles with a fear of failure and is constantly afraid of making mistakes.

Unfortunately, the fear holds her back, causing her to stagnate. It's truly a pity because these times require many brilliant souls to make a difference. Her younger daughter follows our intensive dance training. The mum recognises the same perfectionist tendencies in her younger daughter. This girl learned through dancing that making mistakes is OK. It's a chance to learn and improve.

Her mum told us that if her oldest daughter had also danced, she would probably have been stronger in life today. She regrets not realising the impact back then; perhaps she would turn back time if she could.

Valuing effort over outcome

> 'Hard work beats talent when talent doesn't work hard.'[36]
> — Tim Notke

As parents and educators, our gaze often fixates on the tangible – grades, scores and accolades. There is no doubt of their place in modern society. Yet, equally crucial is our recognition and celebration of the effort and dedication our children invest in their actions. It's the perseverance through challenges, the hard work behind the scenes, and the resilience in the face of setbacks that deserves applause. Operating only with the end destination in mind, means we miss valuable lessons learnt along the way. Life then becomes a series of transactions. Could it be why so many are disillusioned with their work or careers.

By shifting our focus from the end result to the journey itself, we instil a sense of self-confidence in our children. Emphasising the process over the product teaches our children to value growth, learning, and the grit it takes to pursue their goals.

Completing the process (Do it)

If we have set up the previous step correctly (Dream it), then this next step is where the rubber meets the road. This execution phase stands as a test of perseverance, discipline, and the ability to delay gratification. This phase challenges individuals, especially young learners, to apply themselves consistently, even when immediate rewards are not evident.

Discipline and delayed gratification

To navigate the 'process' – whether it's mastering a new dance routine, persevering through difficult piano scales, or sticking with horse riding through less-than-perfect weather – requires discipline and patience.

Let's look at some scenarios.

Your child is excited. She has moved up to a more advanced dance level and the class is rehearsing a new choreography to be performed for a large audience in three months. She's dreaming of being on the stage, wearing those lovely costumes and being the star. It's something 'new' to look forward to.

Weeks go by, the novelty begins to wear off. It turns out that the choreography is not that easy, after all. The child is a little tired and sore. She says one day, 'Mum, is it OK if I skip training?'

Sound familiar? The week thereafter she is behind in the choreography. The teacher is annoyed that she didn't show up. And that important lift she was in has been assigned to another dancer. Damn.

It's that hurdle of still going to training, especially at those times when it's not going so smoothly. It's being able to say 'no' to friends when they ask to get ready together for a friend's birthday party – 'No, because I have dance'. Perseverance and discipline come into play here, to be able to endure.

Here's another scenario.

Meanwhile, another kid wants to do horseriding. After a few lessons, a rainy day makes horseriding less attractive. Ughh, imagine getting all wet in the rain. The piano, now that's more her style. Then the more challenging piano stuff creeps in, where things get a bit trickier, and it becomes a chore.

And so we encounter children who jump from one hobby to another, seduced by the novelty of each new activity without committing to anything. This 'shiny object syndrome' sees kids being constantly distracted by new ideas without finishing current projects. Every new and shiny idea immediately grabs their attention, causing them to lose focus on what they are doing.

As a result, they always stay a beginner.

Delaying gratification has been extensively studied in psychology, most famously in the 'Marshmallow Test' experiment.[37] In this study, young children were given a single marshmallow and were instructed that if they could wait until the researcher returned before they ate it, they would receive a second marshmallow as a reward.

The children who could delay their craving for the marshmallow for the promise of a future reward showed better life outcomes in their adulthood. Not only that, they also achieved higher academic performance and better emotional intelligence. The waiting paid off.

Learning to dance teaches children to focus on long-term goals and endure the discomfort of waiting. This ability to delay gratification will serve them well as they grow into 'good' adults. They will be able to steer their ship better, not succumbing to every whim. They will have a better life trajectory, whether in academia, business or in their personal relationships.

Here are some benefits of teaching delayed gratification to the children:

- **Better grades:** They excel in school because they focus on long-term academic goals.

MENTAL AND EMOTIONAL GROWTH

- **Improved self-control:** They are empowered to make smarter choices and resist impulses.

- **Enhanced resilience:** They demonstrate better problem-solving skills.

- **Healthier relationships:** They show better emotional regulation and social skills.

- **Long-term success:** They are better able to achieve significant life goals, leading to greater fulfilment.

Dance, with its structure, discipline and gradual progress, is a perfect platform. It takes practice and patience to master steps, and waiting for the final show teaches delayed gratification. In dance, there are no shortcuts to success. No quick fix, no magic button. A dance group will train for many hours for a performance that might only last a few minutes. And then it's back to the drawing board for the next performance.

Whether you are a beginner or a student at a top professional dance academy, every dancer starts their practice in the same way, by going to the barre. Back to basics, each day. To warm up it is starting with the plié, day in and day out. It is only in the moments leading up to the performance that it all comes together. It now starts to make sense once the lights, music and choreography blend together.

One mother shared her thoughts with us:

'The discipline instilled in my daughters from their dance lessons shines through in their academic pursuits. They have received numerous compliments from their school teachers on this aspect.'

Reflection and feedback

Congratulations – at this stage, your child has gone through the execution or 'do it' phase. All the dreams, the training, persevering with discipline and patience, and then reaping the rewards of that wonderful experience. Now comes the reflection, the analysis, and the adjustments to start the cycle again, this time armed with more self-awareness and experience.

When your child reflects on their dance performance, it will definitely improve their achievements. It's about pausing, taking a moment to realise what they have learned, and thinking about their next steps. Our competition dancers look forward to the feedback emails. They understand that this feedback can help consolidate their strengths while working on the weaker aspects of their choreography.

Thinking about thinking, also known as metacognition, is crucial for dancers. It involves analysing how they plan, organise and execute their dance. This higher level of thinking makes your child a more efficient learner, leading to improved dance performances and a more profound growth experience.

Processing uncomfortable truths as an accelerator

Giving feedback is invaluable. As dance students ourselves, we found writing about our experiences in a diary helped to increase our self-awareness and encouraged us to seek advice from our teachers. We noted down all the feedback in a diary. Before the class started, we briefly read the feedback. This way, we could enter the dance class with a specific goal in mind, 'Today, I will focus on my arms. Tomorrow, I will pay attention to my connection with the audience.'

Every so often, it's hard to hear 'criticism', but see it as feedback. During our time at the dance academy, we were happy to receive feedback from our teacher. It meant they found it valuable to work with us. Yes, it's actually a compliment.

TIPS FOR PARENTS

Introduce journaling or drawing to your child. In our family we doodle or write about our 'small wins' every day to create self-awareness.

Research shows the value of reflection, as it enhances performance on the dance floor.[38] Similarly, in business, employees who dedicate a few minutes at the end of their working day to reflection outperform their colleagues who do not.

Reflecting helps your child to face their worries, such as comparing themselves to others or recognising negative self-talk, and to take action to change these patterns.

If you have a splinter, you feel the pain. You pause, locate the splinter, remove it (hopefully quickly), then care for the wound and in no time the skin heals. It is a metaphor for using reflection to solve pain points in life, identifying the issue and taking steps to heal and move forward.

But after looking back and dealing with what was, the question still lingers: what's next? The next phase isn't about looking back, but looking forward, taking what we've learned and using it to shape what's next. In looking forward we found something amazing.

What if we told you there's one big truth that can change your everyday life? It's been right in front of us all along, something so basic we've sensed it all along, yet only now understand its power. Imagine waking up every morning with an electric sense of possibility, knowing deep down in your bones what you're about to do really matters. The secret isn't about getting more or going higher. It's about something simpler and more beautiful. It's about creating ripples that go far beyond you, touching lives in ways you may never even see.

It's the path to a life full of meaning and fulfilment.

Passing the baton (Give it)

We always knew we were passionate about our cause, but we struggled to express it. It was the feeling of wanting to get up early for it, stay up late for it and pour every ounce of energy into it. Ultimately, it came down to one thing: making a lasting impact on young people through dance.

In the beginning, we were hesitant to share our expertise. After all, it takes years to master the art of dance, and it's personal, filled with experiences, mistakes and revelations. It was counterintuitive at first – how could giving away knowledge benefit us? But, as we began to share, the ripples went further than we could have imagined. Our videos, blogs, and social media posts became touchpoints of inspiration and connection.

Sharing our expertise magnifies it. It draws people in, attracts talent, builds trust and creates a community of learners. People see us not just as dance teachers but as mentors, guides and partners in their personal growth.

It's in this spirit of sharing that we develop emotional intelligence, which is key to the next generation's success in a world where technology is everywhere and information is cheap. We are raising kids with the ability to apply knowledge in creative and resourceful ways.

Passing the baton – the act of giving – is more than an act of kindness. It's a fundamental skill of emotional intelligence. Emotional intelligence is understanding and managing your emotions while understanding others. Giving means trusting others to use it, to try, to fail and to grow. It is being open enough to know when to let go, to make space for the next person to step up.

Think of Jamie Oliver. He became famous because he shared his recipes freely and changed everyday cooking for people all over the world. He chose an abundance mindset – one that believes in giving, teaching and trusting people to learn and grow. His openness led to better school meals across the country, a food revolution and a multi-million-pound business.

Similarly, Patagonia, an outdoor clothing and gear company, has shown how sharing values and being open can have an impact far beyond what you can imagine. Their mission, 'We're in business to save our home planet' sums up their environmental commitment.[39] Through initiatives like Worn Wear – encouraging customers to repair and recycle gear, or donating 1% of sales to environmental organisations, they have created a blueprint for conscious business that others are now following. Being open hasn't hurt their bottom line – it's increased it while inspiring a generation of conscious consumers.

Patagonia's approach to sharing and openness is a lesson for us as parents. Teaching children to share and help others is a way to make them more understanding, build community and prepare them to be leaders of the world.

Our children need this sense of purpose, to know not just what they are good at, but why they do it. In the conceptual age, where creativity, innovation and connection matter, our children must learn to tap into their internal motivation.

Look at your child. Watch closely to see what gets them lit up. Is it building things? Performing? Helping others? These are the clues to their inner compass. Help them pursue their interests, even if they seem strange.

Try this:

- Set a timer and give your child your full, undivided attention

- Notice one thing they are naturally drawn to and ask them why they love it

- Share a skill you're currently learning – show them adults learn too!

Give your time, your expertise, and even your mistakes to your children. Show them that learning is not just about consuming information, but how they use it. Show them the power of giving back. Whether it's helping with an event or supporting other parents, these acts of giving are more powerful than we realise. Children learn by observing us. If they see us sharing, they will too.

Brain development

Child psychologist Dr. Ann-Louise Lockhart explains the prefrontal cortex – which helps us manage emotions, personality, planning and focus – doesn't fully develop until our twenties.[40] Since children's prefrontal cortex is still growing, they struggle with tasks that are easy for adults. This means they are still learning skills like impulse control, planning and problem-solving. Until this part of the brain is fully developed, parents need to be their child's external brain manager. Understanding this biological fact means we need to be more patient and compassionate. Instead of expecting them to act like mini adults, we have to recognise their brains are growing, and our job is to guide them consistently and gently as they develop these skills.

Training the neural net

Our brains are like neural networks in machine learning, trained through repeated experiences, just like machine learning models are trained with data over and over again to improve.

MENTAL AND EMOTIONAL GROWTH

If children are repeatedly exposed to scarcity thinking – messages of 'not enough', fear and limitation – they will internalise that mindset. On the other hand, if we expose them to a perspective of abundance[41] and possibility, they will learn to approach the world with openness and courage. This is why modelling positive behaviour and a growth mindset is so important. As parents, our actions, and the environment we create become the training data for our children's neural net.

We've seen this in our studio: the most generous performers who don't hesitate to bare themselves get the main roles. The ones who truly care about others get to run the camps so they can be front and centre teaching younger students and nurturing them.

Just as a neural net is shaped by the data it's fed, our children's perspectives are shaped by what they see, hear and experience every day. Encourage positivity, curiosity and resilience, and help them avoid constant exposure to negative influences.

Quick wins:

- Replace 'Be careful!' with 'What do you notice about...?'
- Point out one example of abundance in your daily life
- Share a family photo and tell its story: building positive neural connections

The power of questions

When answers are just a click away, asking good questions is becoming more important than ever. Because when we ask stupid questions, we get stupid answers.

Leaders, thinkers and creators aren't the ones who know everything, but the ones who aren't afraid to ask questions. A curious, questioning mind will thrive in a tech-driven world.

Quick wins:

- Child: Instead of asking a weak question like 'Why can't I do this?', they could reframe it to 'What can I try differently to improve?'

- Parent: Ask 'How was school?' and you'll probably get 'Alright.' Instead, try 'What was the most interesting part of your day?' or 'Did anything surprise you today?'

Summary: Nurturing the next generation

When it comes to raising children, shortcuts often fail to instil the traits we want them to possess. Learning to grow mentally and emotionally, understanding our beliefs, controlling our emotions, and building strength pays off in the long run. A child who is nurtured with patience and perseverance has positive impacts on all those around them and throughout wider society.

Making choices in how we spend time with our children, such as choosing shared meals over screen time and encouraging open communication from a young age, helps build connections and success in the future.

Investing in our children's emotional development is like looking through a magnifying glass: what we choose to nurture gets magnified.

The future demands a generation of young people who are driven by purpose, guided by empathy and unafraid to share.

8
Building Stronger Tribes

Human beings are social animals, dependent on relationships. A sense of belonging is a need that originates from human nature itself. Whether it's family, sports teams, hobbies, spiritual communities, charities, political affiliations, cities, countries or nationalities, our existence revolves around being part of something bigger than ourselves.

Dance classes and groups are a miniature representation of society, where people from diverse backgrounds come together with a common purpose. This shared interest in dance gives a sense of belonging and identity, creating the 'tribe'.

'A village is needed to raise a child', according to an African saying. This phrase emphasises the importance of providing children with a nurturing environment that helps them grow and be well, and the 'village' includes not only family members, but also extended relatives, neighbours, educators, professionals and community members.

In many countries today, the family structure has become fragmented, which has led to more isolation and a reluctance to ask others for help. Family issues, money problems, busy work schedules and moving around more often have caused families to feel disconnected from their communities.

The lessons from the pandemic

We never truly understood the value of human connection until it was suddenly taken away. The pandemic didn't just separate us physically—it highlighted how much we need human touch and presence for our wellbeing.

Parents watched as their once vibrant, social children began to withdraw. Teenagers missed important milestones, and young children—who learn so much through play and physical interaction—were left isolated behind screens. It wasn't that we missed going to the movies or dance classes; it was about losing that irreplaceable human connection we had taken for granted.

When our dance classes moved online, they became lifelines. Students logged in early to chat with friends, and stayed late to share their struggles and hopes with their tribe. Even through a screen, that shared experience gave us the sense of togetherness we all required most.

In a time of uncertainty, having a sense of belonging keeps us grounded.

Building stronger foundations: Hello, thank you, goodbye

Having many people in a room does not make them a tribe. A tribe is forged through shared experiences, values and goals. It's only as strong as the individuals who actively contribute to the group's purpose. To have true social cohesion, we need to develop valuable social skills like active listening and empathy, treating each other with respect and understanding.

There is a trend of increasing shyness among teens, so it is policy in Ndigo for everyone to greet each other with a simple hello when they enter the studio or dressing room. Saying 'thank you' or 'goodbye' at the end of a class, followed by an applause or reverence (curtsy), is also good manners. In ballet, reverence is a bow or curtsy performed to acknowledge the teacher, pianist, orchestra or audience. It is a gesture of respect and appreciation for their presence.

Familiarity breeds indifference: The power of multiple voices

In the studio, we encourage dancers to work with multiple teachers to gain a deeper understanding. Many times, we hear dancers say, 'Oh, Ms X said the same thing'. Same message, different messenger.

When the same message is said by different people, the message hits home. When different members of the community provide similar perspectives, it reinforces important life lessons. This is where the village concept becomes crucial in child-rearing.

Bridging the intergenerational gap

As a child, Justin lived with his parents, grandparents, uncle and aunt, all under one roof. He remembers special times when he felt safe and loved, like a part of the larger family.

The interests, attitudes and abilities of the oldest and youngest generations may today seem distant. However, bridging this gap can offer numerous benefits to both groups. The younger generation can learn from seniors' experience, while seniors can embrace new ideas, technologies and fresh perspectives from younger generations.

We see the impact first-hand when we go to the nursing home called Waterdam near our dance school. It's a beautiful, red-bricked modern retirement home in the middle of the city.

Several times a year, we perform there with our younger dancers, aged three to twelve years old. The interaction between our dancers and residents creates a beautiful connection. The dancers are happy with their work and the audience is interested in them. The older people tap their feet, clap their hands, and sing or hum along. We ask them to perform and execute simple dance moves, and they invariably ask for an 'encore' after each performance. The kids love the attention and everyone wins on that day.

And it benefits the elderly too – music and dance stimulate the brain and body, thereby promoting well-being. Music, particularly, is known to aid memory, especially in those with Alzheimer's or dementia. It is more than just an enjoyable afternoon, though. It brings two generations together, teaching dancers about commitment and contributing to something greater.

Making real impact: From local to global

Dance is a universal language that connects us all. In our studio we see this happen all the time. Choreographers from all over the world join us in

Belgium. Justin remembers a teacher from Japan who spoke very little English, yet within minutes of starting class everyone was moving together, understanding every gesture. What unites us, whether we are from Tokyo or Antwerp, is our love for beauty, expression and creativity. In those moments language becomes secondary.

Children should be raised with this global perspective. How do we raise children who see beyond borders and boundaries? Sadhguru, an Indian mystic, says that when we limit our identity to just family, community or nation we create more divisions. Like a butterfly's wings creating ripples that affect weather patterns on the other side of the world, a child's small act of kindness can create change that goes far much further.[42]

When we cling to limited identities we see others as different and blame them for problems we also contribute to. This 'Us vs Them' mindset fuels conflicts big and small.

Raising a global perspective starts with daily choices: how we talk about other cultures at dinner, the stories we share, the way we explain world events to our children. Every conversation is a chance to help them understand their role in this world and that every choice no matter how small can make a difference.

'You can't connect the dots looking forward; you can only connect them looking backwards.'[43]
— Steve Jobs

GLOCAL = Local businesses, global impact

Work as we know it is changing. Modern technology is expected to take over a significant portion of the workforce, but simultaneously, we're witnessing the rise of creative entrepreneurs with a mission to solve global problems.

We want to be part of this movement. We hopped over to the UN's Sustainable Development Goals website and picked a few goals that we care about.[44] Since we work with children and teens every day, we chose well-being and quality education to start with.

We then connected with B1G1 (Buy 1 Give 1) that supports more than 450 carefully selected and vetted projects that are making a real difference in the lives of people and communities. They provide tools that track the impacts each business has made. This makes it easy to track and gives you control over how much you spend.

Start small, and as your business grows, increase your impact. It's that easy!

A GLOCAL business nurtures its local roots while positioning itself on the global stage. Consider a local craftsman who uses traditional methods to create eco-friendly products, then markets them globally through e-commerce platforms, promoting sustainable consumption worldwide.

In today's interconnected world, new opportunities for collaboration and growth are emerging. A tech startup in a small city might develop an app to improve local public transportation, then adapt and scale their solution for cities around the world by tapping into a global talent pool.

At Ndigo today, we have teachers based in Belgium, but we have a support team based in India and the Philippines. Meetings are conducted on Zoom and work is assigned, tracked and managed in the cloud. We also work with suppliers based in Europe, Australia, United States and China who supply our web store for products that we source globally but for local clients.

By adopting this GLOCAL approach, businesses can have a positive impact both locally and globally, advancing economic growth in their communities while contributing to solving global challenges.

Summary: Establish a global mindset in children

Raising kids to be ready for tomorrow's world means mixing the best of what's right here with the vastness of what's out there. Here are three tips to establish a global mindset in children:

- Encourage them to learn about different countries, languages and traditions by reading books, watching movies and attending cultural events.
- Get your children to think about how global issues affect people around the world by talking about them at the right age.
- Travel with your children. They will learn many things that can't be experienced in a classroom.

Having a global mindset is important because:

- Children are better prepared for an increasingly connected world.
- It encourages empathy, tolerance and understanding of different viewpoints.

- It informs kids how to tackle global problems in the future.

To sum up, it's important to make our communities stronger and teach our children to think globally. By embracing diversity, encouraging intergenerational connections, and thinking globally, we can make a world that is more connected and compassionate for future generations.

Do you want to make an impact? Start here:

- United Nations Sustainable Development Goals website (www.un.org/sustainabledevelopment/sustainable-development-goals/) – provides information and resources on global issues and how to contribute.

- B1G1 – Creating impacts as a business (https://b1g1.com/).

- Global Citizen (www.globalcitizen.org/) offers information on global issues and ways to take action.

9
Hesitations

We've covered the benefits of dance, but you may still have some lingering questions. After years of hearing the same worries, we've identified a few common ones:

- 'Boys don't dance, it's for girls.'
- 'School first, dance is a hobby.'
- 'What if my child gets injured?'
- 'My child doesn't have a dancer's body.'
- 'Dance takes up too much of our time, effort and money.'

Let's look into these concerns, stereotypes, academic balance and why dance is more than just a pastime.

Boys do dance

Billy Elliot is a fictional movie about a boy who wants to be a dancer, despite facing opposition from his family and community. Billy goes through all the common struggles of being the only boy in the dance class surrounded by girls.

His only support comes from his dance teacher, who sees his potential and encourages Billy to audition for the Royal Ballet School. This only happens when Billy's father gives up his ego and throws his full weight behind Billy's dreams. You could say that is the turning point of the story.

Years later, the movie cuts to Billy's father and brother rushing to their seats in the theatre, eager to watch Billy in a lead role. The film ends with his father gasping in awe as Billy takes the stage with an impressive leap.

Another, more recent, movie is *Yeh Ballet* on Netflix, which is based on the true story of two boys from the slums of Mumbai. Both have tons of talent but need a platform to showcase their talents internationally.

Enter seventy-year-old real-life ballet teacher Yehuda Maor, who works at The (real) Danceworx academy to promote classical ballet in India. Yehuda personally takes the dancers under his wing, providing them with training, support, and connecting them to audition committees overseas. Today, both dancers (real names: Amiruddin Shah and Manish Chauhan) are in the United Kingdom and United States respectively and are professional dancers living their dream.

Justin has a personal connection to this story, he explains:

> '*Yeh Ballet* is closer to home for me as it's about two dancers who have trained in The Danceworx. It was the same dance school where I started dancing under the guidance of Ashley Lobo. Had it not been for his vision to promote dance in India, I probably wouldn't be here writing this book.
>
> 'I consider myself lucky to be part of the original batch of The Danceworx when there were no role models, no success stories and dance as a career was only a pipe dream. Ashley tells me regularly that he's proud we made it in dance. It's because of our success in introducing Western dance styles in India that there's a considerable influx of male dancers from India.
>
> 'I've only met Yehuda once, but he also left a deep impact on me. Both teachers are highly recognised and highly praised, but it was their physical, emotional and mental support that encouraged dancers like myself to take up dance as a career.'

Today's reality

Sadly, family and community opposition is still a reality for many boys who want to dance, even in Western developed countries – lack of support, or even worse, bullying, are commonplace. There are plenty of dance schools with the right infrastructure, training methodologies and plenty of companies that put up shows in local theatres.

But it's still not widely accepted for men to dance, and especially in specific dance styles that are considered feminine in the West. This perception hinders male dancers' interest in dance.

We believe it is not the lack of infrastructure or access to good teachers, but the personal motivation of the dancer and a lack of support at home and in their communities.

Stereotyping

There is the deeply ingrained stereotype that dance is a feminine activity. Many cultures, including Belgian culture, believe that boys should not dance because they fear being judged or ridiculed. Boys don't dance because they worry about how their friends and adults will see them.

Many parents are also worried about what others in their community might think of them if their son would be dancing. There are modern, well-educated families that have this nagging fear that their son might 'become gay' just because he's dancing, and thus get 'infected' by such practices.

We do have some boys in toddler dance. The boys have fun dancing and are excited to come to class. They will even perform at the end-of-year recital. At a certain point around the age of six is when a student has more options open up for them. Students can choose to enrol in styles like ballet, jazz or urban dance. Yet, there is an opposite effect. Most boys at this stage drop out. It's a strange thing, but we've seen it many times.

On another occasion, we were pleasantly surprised to have a boy in a summer camp one year. The boy was very talented. He had a good sense of the music and body coordination. The teacher in charge gave the boy the lead role and he did a fantastic job during the performance.

After the camp, the boy asked his mum to enrol him in regular classes during the year. Sadly, his mum replied, 'Sorry, we only wanted a camp to keep you busy during the holidays while we are at work; and besides, what would your dad say?'

We never saw him again.

Brave male dancers

To be a male dancer, you must either be extremely brave or foolhardy. With so few male dancers in dance classes, it's a tough road.

To survive in dance, a male dancer must have the following characteristics (otherwise, it will be death by a thousand cuts, usually out of fear, judgement, ignorance and ego):

- He should be a pioneering spirit.
- He must be oblivious to the comments he will surely receive.
- He must be determined, and focus only on himself.
- He will need the support of his elders.

The National Ballet of Canada

It's not all doom and gloom for boys dancing. On a more positive note, in 2020, The National Ballet of Canada announced that there would be more boys than girls graduating. The class had sixteen guys and eleven girls. Such stories need to be shared more often.

One thing to note is that dance schools like this have strong outreach programmes to reach out to the youth. If the boys don't come into a dance class, the school will have to go to them. This is sometimes in the form of visiting schools, but they also invite the public behind the scenes to witness professional rehearsals or to talk about the choreographic process. They excel in the use of social media, blog posts and videos to show how boys can thrive once they are in a supportive environment.

The National Ballet even offers performances to over 110,000 people for free.

Other ballet and contemporary companies will have similar programmes aimed at connecting with their communities and making dance more accessible and familiar. For many parents, taking their children to a dance performance isn't always easy—tickets can be expensive, schedules are often tight, and keeping young children interested throughout the show can be challenging. These outreach programmes help bridge that gap by making the experience more accessible, welcoming and family-friendly.

These initiatives also help break down the idea that dance and theatre are only for a select few. They invite everyone to be a part of the arts, helping bring communities together and making performances a normal and enjoyable experience for all families.

Importantly, these programmes play a key role in exposing children to art and culture they might not otherwise experience. Such exposure can spark creativity and nurture a lifelong appreciation for the performing arts, beginning at a young age.

Advice for parents of a male dancer

While it applies to both parents, it is especially important for dads to attend their sons' performances, to bring them to competitions and classes, and talk to them about their dance journey. Show complete support to your son's decision. You will make a lasting impact on your son.

The negative comments will come. Be proactive in reframing and defending your son from the bullies. A strong father figure will provide the necessary armour for the long run. It's about your son's happiness. Give him the top priority.

Focus on the mental and emotional strength of your child to handle bullying. Teach them that no one is entitled to dictate how they feel from the inside. We may have no control on what others say, but we have full control over how we feel.

Role models for boys

Another thing to consider is representation. In the early history of dance, it was an art form exclusively performed by males, with women not being allowed to participate. This changed during the Romantic period of the late eighteenth and early nineteenth centuries, when female dancers were permitted to take the stage. Over time, they came to dominate the roles in ballet, while male dancers were often relegated to supporting roles.

There is still a lack of visibility in local dance schools. It makes boys think dance isn't for them because they don't see enough male role models.

In contrast to this situation in the local schools, in the professional world, we are now seeing increasing numbers of beautiful male dancers. We are confident that they will influence the next generation of dancers. One only needs to conduct a search on social media platforms to see how amazing these male dancers are.

Sander Blommaert

We had a chance to chat with Sander Blommaert. He is a Belgian dancer and former first soloist at the Royal Ballet Company in the UK. Growing up in his native Bruges, he had little exposure to male dancers from other parts of the world. It wasn't until Sander moved to the UK at fifteen that his world opened up.

Sander's journey wasn't easy. He was bullied and called names, often before he even knew what they meant. Despite all this, he was determined to succeed. He used the opposition he faced as fuel to push himself harder. Today, as founder of Blommaert Ballet School and Ballet-On-Demand, Sander shares his experience with young male students to help them navigate the same challenges and to stay focused on their goals: 'All the opposition just fuelled me to do better. It never got me upset.'

He believes a lot of the concerns parents have about their sons dancing comes from a lack of knowledge. He advises parents to educate themselves about the reality of dance, especially the equality of male and female dancers in professional companies. Whether it's dance or football, he says, supporting your child in their passion is what really matters.

And then there's the fear some parents have that if their son dances, he'll be gay. Sander addresses this head-on, saying sexual orientation is not determined by a person's hobbies or career choices. He explains that, in the dance industry, there's a safe and accepting environment regardless of your sexual orientation. Sander explains that parents who are worried about this should focus on the joy and fulfilment their child finds in dance, not the unfounded fears.

We think it's important to support your child in what they like. Others might say mean things, but it's about how you react that matters. You can't control what someone else is doing, thinking or saying.

Perfect dancing body: A myth

Parents tell us, with the best of intentions, that their child doesn't have a 'perfect dancing body'. Usually, a nice way of saying their child is overweight. This reflects deeper societal pressures, but we believe in a recreational setting dance should be for everyone. Movement is a path to health regardless of body type.

Ineke's personal experience shows how damaging body criticism can be. In her first week at dance academy, she was told by her teacher that she had 'legs like pudding'. Ineke says, 'Thankfully I loved myself enough to handle it. I was OK with who I was and how I looked. Our body is our greatest asset, and we only get one. We must treat it right with nourishing food, proper rest, hydration and consistent strengthening.'

Not everyone has that resilience, and those comments can leave scars for life. The dance environment can exacerbate body image concerns in many ways:

- Mirrored studios mean dancers see and compare themselves to others all the time
- Competitive environments create pressure to have an 'ideal' body type
- Puberty's physical changes are more challenging under constant scrutiny

- Teachers' words carry a lot of weight and can impact body image for years
- Social media amplifies unrealistic beauty standards with filtered perfect images

These pressures often affect dancers' relationship with food. While the dancers can't instantly grow longer legs or a more flexible back, food intake feels controllable and some go down a dangerous path. Eating disorders including anorexia, bulimia and others affect dancers of all genders. The myth that this is a 'female issue' prevents many male dancers from seeking help, despite one third of diagnosed cases being male.

Parents and teachers must create a supportive environment. While specific advice on eating disorders requires professional expertise, we can promote healthy attitudes by:

- Celebrating different body types and their strengths
- Focusing on what bodies can do, not how they look
- Talking openly about body image concerns
- Being aware of the warning signs of disordered eating
- Supporting dancers through physical changes
- Seeking help early if concerns arise

HESITATIONS

Dance is about expression, strength and joy – not fitting into a box

I'm beautiful...

FOR PARENTS

Imagine a mother who constantly says things like 'I don't look pretty', or, 'This skirt makes me look fat', within the hearing of her young daughter. When this girl reaches puberty, it is likely she will have developed a poor body image, and in a worst-case scenario, she may develop an eating disorder or other conditions that may force her to stop doing the things she previously enjoyed, like dancing.

Parents, your words matter. Help your child develop a healthy body image by modelling self-acceptance and positivity.

The risk of injuries

Jee-Eun Petitqueux is an experienced dance pedagogue at the Royal Ballet School of Antwerp. She was also a ballet dancer with the Universal Ballet Company in Seoul and she holds various degrees including psychology for gifted children, sports psychology and EFT (Emotional Freedom Techniques).

We interviewed Jee-Eun, in which she stressed the importance of being in tune with your body. 'Everyone is different,' she said. 'You need to pay attention to your child's physicality.' Seeing professionals such as physiotherapists or osteopaths regularly can help, especially when the body is growing and vulnerable.

A healthy diet and supporting mental health are also key. The mind-body connection is powerful: mental stress can manifest physically, and dancers should be aware of exhaustion, persistent pain or emotional strain as signs of overexertion.

Jee-Eun advises on prevention rather than cure. Injuries can be reduced by proper warm-ups, cool-downs and cross-training. But injury is never far away. When it strikes, it's challenging to fully prepare for its emotional impact. It becomes just as important to recover mentally as it is physically.

Learning to acknowledge your frustrations and work through them is important because the body might recover, but the mind can keep struggling. Accepting setbacks takes resilience.

Jee-Eun says, 'Know yourself as a person and as a dancer. This will help you anticipate and adjust. Listen to your body.'

TIPS FOR PARENTS

- Get help from the right doctors and follow their advice.
- Engage with your child, truly listen, validate their emotions and ask what they need.
- Encourage them to remain part of the process. Observe classes and rehearsals.

Dance is more than 'just a hobby'

'I've been working with a shy girl,' Ineke shares. 'She was so anxious she couldn't answer questions in class. But through our dance lessons, something wonderful happened. She started to open up. Bit by bit, her confidence grew – not just in dance, but in her regular classes too. Even her school results are getting better.'

We often hear parents say that 'Dance is just a hobby', suggesting that it is something easily given up when other priorities arise. While that's a personal choice, it often shows a lack of understanding about dance's true value. We're not claiming that dance solves all of life's problems, but we've seen how it enriches children's lives and even helps them do better in school. It prepares your child for life's challenges, and builds the skills they'll need in the future, perhaps in ways you haven't thought about yet.

In our interview, Sander Blommaert adds that 'A lot of dancers become self-starters or entrepreneurs. You have to promote yourself and your art. Being an artist means wearing many hats.'

Life will throw stressful situations at your children – giving presentations, taking exams or applying for jobs. You won't always be there to guide them. Through dance, your children will learn to face these challenges on their own.

The skills they gain could take them far. In the short term, dance can help with school performance and social confidence. Eventually, though, these skills could lead to success in other professions. Some dancers go on to become marketing professionals, event planners, physical therapists, fitness coaches, doctors, teachers or public speakers.

Why dancers make great leaders

In our studio, we've seen how dance prepares children for leadership roles. It boosts their confidence and equips them to face life's challenges head-on.

At Ndigo, teenage dancers are given regular opportunities, under the guidance of a professional, to develop their leadership skills. A dance camp is the perfect moment to work with younger children. The teens guide the younger ones through activities, play and dance training. They have to comfort the younger children in case they don't feel well or are sad. The leadership team also has to understand their tasks, execute on them and provide feedback. Such qualities prepare our students for the future, to be adaptable, resilient and empathetic leaders, ready for tomorrow.

Dancers make great leaders for many reasons:

- **Multitasking:** Dancers are naturals when it comes to managing multiple things at the same time. Remembering the choreography, executing the fine movements, and keeping a cool head is their strength. This ability to focus on the big picture and the details at the same time shows they can handle multiple aspects of a project or team at the same time.

- **Diversity:** As stated in Chapter 8, dance groups are made up of a diverse range of people and unite individuals of differing ages, backgrounds and personalities. Leaders need skills to guide types of people in their team.

- **Confidence:** Leadership often means being in the public eye, and dancers are no strangers to this. They are used to standing in front of others and performing.

Frequently asked dance questions

We've explored how dance is for everyone – boys and girls alike – and talked about overcoming injuries and developing a positive body image. We've also seen how dance can be more than just a hobby, influencing areas like school performance by building confidence and discipline.

However, we know there are still many more questions that parents often have about dance and its impact. Let us help you by answering some of them here.

1. **How do you balance dance school with other activities?**

Time management and planning is key to balancing dance education with academics. Consider your child's school hours, homework and other commitments when scheduling dance classes.

Encourage your child to use a colour-coded calendar or planner to manage their time effectively. This helps them balance their activities and teaches them valuable planning and time management skills.

2. **What are the career options for professional dancers?**

While becoming a professional dancer is the dream for many, the reality is that only a very small number will get to do that.

Aside from being a professional dancer, you can become a choreographer, teacher or studio owner. Many dancers also find careers in dance therapy, arts administration or dance photography.

The skills learned from dance, such as discipline, teamwork and creativity, are highly valued in many industries. Former dancers excel in event planning, fitness instruction like Pilates or Gyro tonics, or any career that requires strong interpersonal skills and physical awareness.

3. **How can parents help their kids learn to dance if they don't know how to dance themselves?**

You don't need personal dance experience to support your child's dance education. Look for good dance teachers who care, and go to dance events or workshops with your child. During the holidays, go to dance intensives in other schools and locations. It's a great way to meet new dancers, like-minded parents, and teachers. It will broaden your perspectives and lower the emotional barriers if you connect to other like-minded parents.

Use online resources, like www.dance-masterclass.com, read dance blogs and follow dance communities on social media to learn more. Most importantly, be interested in your child's progress and attend all their performances and events. Your involvement and support will mean everything to your child.

4. Is serious dance training expensive?

Serious dance training is a big financial commitment. Costs include regular classes, private coaching, dance attire, shoes and potentially travel for competitions or intensives. Going to a reputable school with a well-rounded curriculum and skilled teachers likely costs more than intensives in a local dance school. However, you will also have access to better teachers, facilities and performance opportunities.

To manage costs, look into scholarship opportunities like Youth America Grand Prix, which can provide partial or full funding for intensives or year-round training. Look for package deals like 'Back to school' promotions or seasonal discounts from dance stores on attire and shoes. Some second-hand options are available for costumes.

The benefits of personal growth and skill development are difficult to measure, even though the cost is high.

5. Will teenage dancers still have time to do something else?

The social interactions a child has with dance depends on their level of involvement. For recreational students, dance can enhance their social life, a space to make friends with like-minded people and still have time for other social activities.

HESITATIONS

For serious dancers, those in competitive or pre-professional programmes, dance will require more time commitment and may limit social activities. But these dancers often form close communities within their dance schools and at competitions or intensives. They develop strong friendships with peers who share their passion and work ethic, and frequently form friendships that go beyond the studio.

6. **What's the role of technology in modern dance education?**

Technology is becoming more and more important in dance education. Some aspects of training can now be done online, like private lessons, master classes and even full courses.

Technology today lets us watch high-quality dance performances and competitions through live streams or recordings. Events like World Ballet Day streamed live on YouTube provide free access to the most famous dance companies that can inspire and educate young dancers. Parents can encourage their children to take advantage of these resources and watch and discuss performances together.

7. **What are the cultural implications of dancing for families from diverse backgrounds?**

Dance is a universal language that crosses cultural boundaries, and it's a great way for children to connect with different groups of people. Dance can broaden one's cultural horizons, and expose dancers to different traditions, music and movement styles from around the world.

Dance is a great opportunity for cultural exchange and understanding, which will help young dancers become more inclusive and aware of the world around them.

8. **How does dance education change as children get older? What should parents expect at each stage?**

Dance education becomes more intense as children get older. For younger children, classes might take place once or twice a week, and focus on basic movements and having fun. As they progress, the frequency and duration of classes will increase, and the technique will become more demanding.

For parents, this means a growing commitment of time and support. In the early years, parents may need to transport their child to and from classes and attend recitals. As dancers get more serious, parents may find themselves travelling to competitions or intensives, sometimes even to other countries.

The financial commitment may also increase with age as more serious training means more classes, private lessons or special programmes. Older dancers may be able to travel independently, though, which will ease some logistical burden on parents.

To manage these changing commitments, consider connecting with other parents to share experiences and possibly carpool. You can adjust the level of commitment to suit your family's needs and your child's goals in dance. Chapter Four has additional information about the different stages of development.

Summary: Some reassurance

It's clear that the journey of a dancer is full of challenges and great rewards. We've tackled the common concerns about dance education, from male dancers to injuries and dance being viewed as 'just a hobby'. We've shared stories, spoken to experts and given advice on how dancing can change young lives.

We know that parents have doubts and questions when considering dance education for their children. The financial and time investment can be big, especially if you are considering the very top institutions of dance. To be honest, only a tiny percentage of dancers will become a professional performer, gaining contracts in the top dance companies. Most of the dancers we are referring to only dance recreationally. In that case, the amount of dance classes can be increased or decreased to cater to your financial needs.

The important thing is to recognise the many benefits of dance for your family:

- It will teach your child valuable life skills.
- It will give your child direction in life.
- Your child will appreciate your support and presence.
- It will strengthen the bond between you and your child.
- It will be a healthy outlet for self-expression and emotional growth.

Your role as parents is invaluable. Your support, encouragement and involvement can make all the difference in your child's dance experience. So embrace the journey, celebrate the small wins, and watch your child grow as a person.

10
Dance And The Future

The Ancient Greek philosopher Heraclitus said, 'No one steps in the same river twice, for it's not the same river, and he's not the same man'.

Unless you've been living under a rock, you'll have noticed that everyone is talking about the rapid rate of change all around us. Be it in technology, workplace dynamics, healthcare, transportation, education, retail, manufacturing, entertainment and even society as a whole, things seem to be changing all at the same time. Common refrains that come up are, 'The world is changing faster than ever', 'It's difficult to keep up' and 'Things aren't the way they used to be'.

With change comes the struggle to adapt. This change isn't a gentle stream but a torrent, more akin to water gushing from a fire hose. According to futurist Ray Kurzweil, the changes we'll see in the upcoming years may be bigger than any humanity has experienced in the past 20,000 years, so hang on.[45] It's as if we're all strapped onto a rocket hurtling towards an unknown future.

The latest World Economic Forum Global Risks Report 2024 identifies the following as some top risks in the coming ten years:[46]

1. Economic risks: The concentration of strategic resources and disruptions to critical infrastructure.

2. Environmental risks: Adverse climate change events, pollution and biodiversity loss.

3. Geopolitical risks: Interstate armed conflicts, terrorist attacks and geoeconomic confrontation.

4. Societal risks: Pandemics, involuntary migration, polarisation and unemployment.

5. Technological risks: Misinformation, disinformation, adverse outcomes from the use of AI, censorship and surveillance.

Our aim isn't to frighten you, it is to arm you. These challenges are indeed global in nature, meaning that everyone will be affected. The time of isolated issues impacting only specific communities, villages or streets has passed.

DANCE AND THE FUTURE

'There is nothing either good or bad, but thinking makes it so.'[47]
— William Shakespeare

There is, therefore, a case for optimism and a positive outcome to all of this. If we are entering the age of abundance, there will be many positive developments on multiple fronts:

- Massive productivity and efficiency: Technology and software can streamline processes.

- Innovation: New products, new services and businesses will arise.

- Communication: Distance will become irrelevant with the use of video and messaging apps.

- Improved healthcare: With new breakthroughs in research, we may yet discover new methods to once and for all defeat chronic and life-threatening diseases, and improve longevity and quality of life.

- Better access to education: High-quality education and access that can be personalised will lift education levels everywhere to give every child an equal chance of success.

- Global challenges: Tackling challenges like climate change and pollution will have to be dealt together on a global level.

From tradition to transformation

To understand where we are going, we should first have a look at where we come from.

As each generation becomes a parent, they want to pass on their wisdom to their children. But the rate of change in the modern world means that each new generation has different challenges and opportunities.

Children nowadays are asked their opinions on every front, whereas our grandparents would have said, 'Don't speak when adults are talking'. One might borrow some lessons from their elders, yet something is likely to change. Change is a rebellion against how things were done, and this disruption is essential for growth.

Parental advice has evolved with each generation, reflecting changing values and societal norms:

- Baby Boomers, with their focus on perseverance and traditional career paths, might advise that you 'Work hard, and you'll succeed'.
- Generation X, valuing self-reliance, might suggest that you 'Trust yourself and take care of your own'.
- Millennials, emphasising personal fulfilment, are likely to encourage you to 'Follow your passion'.

The advice changes with each generation, and so do the words used to express it.

The search for balance

As a modern parent, you want a good work-life balance, seeking jobs that offer both good pay and fulfilment. You are aware that mental health is important for your personal development, and you prioritise this.

Raising your children, you're likely to emphasise individuality and creativity. Additionally, you may focus on developing confidence based on your child's unique strengths.

The planet's future is also on your mind as you think about the world your kids will inherit. Problems like climate change are real. As different parts of the world get affected with droughts, floods, fires and storms, entire populations will be forced to migrate. And as society gets more diverse, you have to figure out how to teach your children about inclusivity, tolerance and equality in a world where conversations about race and gender identity are complicated and often contentious.

You also realise that this is a quite unfamiliar world from the one you grew up in. Technology overload worries you because it affects mental health. The amount of screen time raises concerns about your children living sedentary lifestyles. You encourage them to exercise regularly and get them involved in sports and other physical activities, but it's getting harder to keep young children away from their phones and other devices.

You're aware of the security and safety issues in our connected world. Bullying now extends beyond the playground and into the cyber world. You want to keep your children safe from online predators and inappropriate content, all while worrying about their privacy.

Parenting today is challenging. You are making decisions that your parents never had to face. The fact that you are still reading this book until the end shows you are keen to learn more and do better.

The danger and the opportunity

A big part of the risk of the internet comes from being connected 24/7. Next to the real world, there is a parallel virtual world where your online life leaves a lasting mark. Every time you use the internet or your mobile, it's like you're leaving footprints that can be followed.

The same gadgets can make our kids addicted to screens, making it tough for them to socialise, sleep, or work out. Ironically, the technology meant to connect us has made children feel isolated. Constantly comparing themselves on social media doesn't help either. There are all these extra pressures now making kids feel stressed, anxious and sad.

Today, a child is not raised solely by their parents, but also by the internet. The internet contains all of mankind's information. While this should be positive, there is also lots of garbage information also that shouldn't be shared with children. Extreme violence, torture and porn are not meant for young minds. So-called influencers that dish out nonsensical information is also another danger, next to 'fake news'. The problem is the accessibility of the internet from anywhere. The big bosses of tech and social media companies often talk about not giving their children a smartphone with access to the internet. Maybe we should take heed.

Information is powerful – it can help kids learn, be creative and talk to people all over the world. The tricky bit is learning to use this power safely. Some will learn to use the internet wisely. They will see it as a way to learn new skills and share their creations and ideas with everyone around the world. But others might become just passive users, endlessly scrolling through TikTok or Instagram for entertainment and to pass time. Thus, we'll end up with two groups: those who create and learn, and those who only consume.

Which group would you want your child to be in? The goal is to teach our children how to use technology in a smart way that lives up to one's core values. To figure out what these core values are, you need to look within and do some soul-searching.

Looking within

When adults first arrive at our yoga class, they often come with certain expectations. They expect physical activity and mental stimulation but shy away from self-reflection. They hope the class isn't too spiritual and they often say, 'I'm not that kind of person'. Even if they did try to meditate, some people have trouble closing their eyes.

Closing our eyes forces us to look inside, and many find this unsettling. It's like they fear the dark: not only the absence of light, but the idea of being alone with their thoughts. Questions and reflections may come up that they'd prefer not to face. It's easier to avoid examining yourself.

As our yoga students progress, the quiet moments of reflection become their favourite parts of the class. They walk out of class radiating an afterglow. It's as if they look lighter. This journey of self-discovery isn't unique to yoga, though. Dancers, too, are well-versed in this kind of introspection. In fact, there's a natural parallel between the two disciplines.

Like yogis, dancers are attuned to their bodies and minds, constantly asking questions and listening to their inner selves. Both yogis and dancers discover that they are the only ones responsible for their inner peace. This inner calm can be accessed daily and provides a reset from the outside world.

So why wait?

Why avoid looking inward until we're too burnt out, bored or physically exhausted to find this inner peace? Looking inward offers a way to disconnect from the constant stimuli that bombard our senses. We've become addicted to the dopamine hits of excitement and stimulation, leading to burnout and exhaustion.

Practices like self-reflection, mindfulness and meditation can help us feel calm again. By digging deeper into our inner world, we can find our purpose and learn to live in alignment with our true selves instead of constantly looking for external validation. This journey is not easy. Your inner voice is often just a whisper.

Choose to listen to it or choose to ignore it.

Why is it important to find alignment?

Have you ever met someone who has a deep sense of purpose? Everything they do has a drive and sense of clarity. These people have found their mission. A mission so aligned that there is no struggle or doubt.

Now imagine you have found your mission. What impact would that have on you? Would that help you find activities, jobs or interactions that have more purpose than mere entertainment? By connecting deeply with yourself, you develop a sense of compassion, empathy and responsibility for others, shifting the focus from an individualistic, even selfish, kind of success, to collective well-being.

In a world where AI and technology can replicate many human tasks and even mimic human intelligence, the need to turn inward has never been more important. The risk of misinformation and disinformation is considerable because information can now be altered via video, audio and text, influencing entire populations. Deepfakes can easily be created, and they are cheap enough to scale infinitely. If everything outside of us can be mimicked, the question is: what is real?

The answer lies within us.

TIPS FOR PARENTS

Encourage your kids to try the following:

- **Breathe:** Pay attention to your breathing. Try to breathe out slowly. This helps your body and mind relax, and can calm your thoughts and feelings.
- **Get outside:** Spend time in nature. Go for a walk in a park or sit under a tree. Being in nature can help you feel calm and more connected to yourself.

- **Write it down:** Keep a journal. Write down your thoughts and feelings. This can help you understand yourself better and work through problems.
- **Enjoy art:** Listen to music, look at paintings, or try making something yourself. Art can help you express and understand your feelings in new ways.
- **Dance:** Try dancing or just moving to music. This can help you express yourself and feel more, and it benefits your body and mind.

Summary: The time is now

Today, right now, we invite you to move. Not for an audience, not for social media, but for yourself. Put on your favourite song and start moving. Feel awkward? Good. That's growth happening.

Dance is a path inward in a world obsessed with external accomplishments. It is your chance to remove the labels that society places on you. You are a mother, a father, a CEO, a salesman, whatever, it doesn't matter. Who are you actually, beneath these roles? After removing these labels, you'll find no label can define you entirely. So why put finite labels on our children as well? Because children are a possibility.

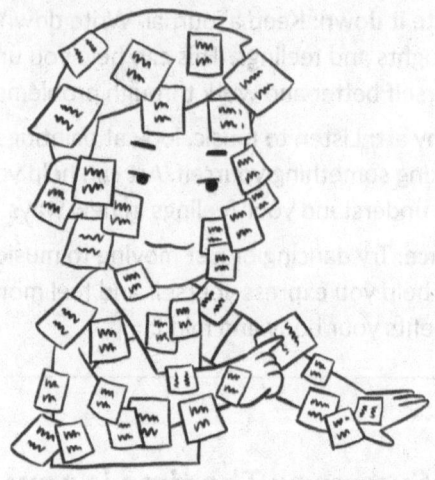

A possibility to become anything.

Our son Milan remarks, 'When I dance, I truly feel like myself'. And thus, he wants to make dance his career. Incredibly brave to have such determination and purpose.

And so, the time to explore your authentic self is now. Dream big by expanding your horizons, then take massive action, and, finally, make an impact by giving back to the world.

It all starts with you. Dream it, Do it, Give it...

Notes

1 Chini, M, 'One in five adults in Flanders has serious psychological problems', *The Brussels Times* (7 February 2024), www.brusselstimes.com/912514/one-in-five-adults-in-flanders-has-serious-psychological-problems, accessed 4 November 2024
2 Mostaque, E, 'How To Think About AI', Schelling AI (31 July, 2024), https://schellingai.substack.com/p/how-to-think-about-ai, accessed 3 December 2024
3 OECD, 'Managing screen time: How to protect and equip students against distraction: PISA in Focus, No 124' (OECD Publishing, 2024), https://doi.org/10.1787/7c225af4-en, accessed 5 October 2024

4 World Economic Forum, 'The Future of Jobs Report 2020' (2020), www3.weforum.org/docs/WEF_Future_of_Jobs_2020.pdf, accessed 12 October 2024
5 Ritchie, G, *Aladdin* (Walt Disney Pictures, 2019)
6 World Economic Forum, 'The Future of Jobs Report 2020' (2020), www3.weforum.org/docs/WEF_Future_of_Jobs_2020.pdf, accessed 12 October 2024
7 Admin, 'Bhimbetka: A glimpse into the earliest traces of human life on the Indian subcontinent', Art Fervour (2 December 2019), https://artfervour.com/bhimbetka-a-glimpse-into-the-earliest-traces-of-human-life-on-the-indian-subcontinent, accessed 4 November 2024
8 Frishchen, U, Degé, F and Schwarzer, G, 'The relation between rhythm processing and cognitive abilities during child development: The role of prediction', Frontiers in Psychology (23 September 2022), www.frontiersin.org/journals/psychology/articles/10.3389/fpsyg.2022.920513/pdf, accessed 4 November 2024
9 Brown, S and Parsons, L, 'The Neuroscience of Dance', *Scientific American* (July 2008), https://neuroarts.org/pdf/SciAm_Dance.pdf, accessed 4 November 2024
10 Complicité, 'Figures in Extinction [1.0]' (2023), www.youtube.com/watch?v=pmOwwelafag, accessed 4 November 2024

NOTES

11 vrt, 'The number of unfilled vacancies in education up 20% on this time last year', vrt nws (8 August 2023), www.vrt.be/vrtnws/en/2023/08/08/the-number-of-unfilled-vacancies-in-education-up-20-on-this-tim/, accessed 4 November 2024

12 World Economic Forum, 'The Future of Jobs Report 2023' (2023), www.weforum.org/agenda/2023/05/future-of-jobs-2023-skills, accessed 4 November 2024

13 OpenExO, 'Building a business for the Future?' (2023), www.youtube.com/watch?v=df7hm1RfLI&t=7209s, accessed 4 November 2024

14 AFZ, 'Eastman Kodak: From Market Leader to Bankruptcy', Harvard Business School, Technology And Operations Management: MBA Student Perspectives (7 December 2015), https://d3.harvard.edu/platform-rctom/submission/eastman-kodak-from-market-leader-to-bankruptcy, accessed 4 November 2024

15 Mondrian, P and Beekman, EM (translator), *Natural Reality and Abstract Reality* (George Braziller Inc, 1995)

16 Bommerez, J, *Minder moeten, meer FLOW* (Uitgeverij MultiLibris, 2022)

17 Viereck, GS, 'What Life Means to Einstein: An Interview' by George Sylvester Viereck, *The Saturday Evening Post* (26 October 1926), p.117, www.saturdayeveningpost.com/wp-content/uploads/satevepost/einstein.pdf, accessed 4 November 2024

18 Robinson, K, 'Do schools kill creativity?' (2007), www.youtube.com/watch?v=iG9CE55wbtY, accessed 4 November 2024
19 Land, G and Jarman, B, *Breakpoint and Beyond: Mastering the Future Today* (Leadership 2000 Inc, 1998)
20 Warren, F, et al, 'The role of implicit theories, age, and gender in the creative performance of children and adults', Thinking Skills and Creativity (June 2018), www.sciencedirect.com/science/article/abs/pii/S1871187117303516?via%3Dihub, accessed 4 November 2024
21 ABT Medical Advisory Board, *The Healthy Dancer: ABT Guidelines for Dancer Heath* (Macfadden Performing Arts Medi, 2008)
22 Cappelaere, G, 'The Mental Health Burden Affecting Europe's Children', UNICEF (4 October 2021), www.unicef.org/eu/stories/mental-health-burden-affecting-europes-children, accessed 4 November 2024
23 Peck, S, *The Road Less Travelled* (Arrow, 1990)
24 Harvard University, *Resilience* (The Center on the Developing Child, no date), https://developingchild.harvard.edu/science/key-concepts/resilience/, accessed 12 October 2024
25 Harvard Medical School, 'In a slump? Fix your posture', Harvard Health Publishing (no date), www.health.harvard.edu/staying-healthy/in-a-slump-fix-your-posture, accessed 4 November 2024

NOTES

26 Robbins, T, 'Are you sending the wrong signals?' (no date), www.tonyrobbins.com/blog/are-you-sending-the-wrong-signals, accessed 4 November 2024

27 Harvard Medical School, 'In a slump? Fix your posture', Harvard Health Publishing (no date), www.health.harvard.edu/staying-healthy/in-a-slump-fix-your-posture, accessed 4 November 2024

28 Royal Ballet School, Enlighten Webinar (The Healthy Dancer) for Stretching and Flexibility, www.royalballetschool.org.uk/2020/09/24/the-royal-ballet-school-launches-enlighten-teacher-training-webinars, accessed 4 November 2024

29 Nair, S, et al, 'Do slumped and upright postures affect stress responses? A randomized trial', *Health Psychology* (September 2015), https://pubmed.ncbi.nlm.nih.gov/25222091, accessed 4 November 2024

30 Cunningham, S, 'Increased use of screen time causing back pain in kids', UCHealth Today (7 December 2023), www.uchealth.org/today/increased-use-of-screen-time-causing-back-pain-in-kids, accessed 4 November 2024

31 Earhart, G, 'Dance as Therapy for Individuals with Parkinson Disease', European Journal of Physical and Rehabilitation Medicine (June 2009), https://pmc.ncbi.nlm.nih.gov/articles/PMC2780534, accessed 4 November 2024

32 Hyman, Ira, PhD, 'Listening to Music and Watching Dance Using Mirror Neurons', Psychology Today (9 August 2012), www.

psychologytoday.com/intl/blog/mental-mishaps/201208/listening-music-and-watching-dance-using-mirror-neurons, accessed 4 November 2024

33 Routhier, S, *Top 20 Most Physically Demanding Jobs* (Insurance Providers, 2024), www.insuranceproviders.com/most-physically-demanding-jobs/, accessed 12 October 2024

34 Jensen, A, 'Johann Wolfgang von Goethe (1749–1832)', Internet Encyclopedia of Philosophy (no date), https://iep.utm.edu/goethe, accessed 4 November 2024

35 Latimore, E (@EdLatimore), 'Embarrassment is the cost of entry…' (2 November 2018), https://x.com/EdLatimore/status/1058305553020141570?lang=en, accessed 4 November 2024

36 Klein, D, 'Hard Work Beats Talent…', By David Klein (17 May 2021), www.bydavidklein.com/2021/05/17/hard-work-beats-talent, accessed 4 November 2024

37 Mischel, W and Ebbesen, EB, 'Attention in delay of gratification', *Journal of Personality and Social Psychology*, 16/2, 329–337, doi.org/10.1037/h0029815

38 Bailey, J and Rehman, S, 'Don't Underestimate the Power of Self-Reflection', *Harvard Business Review* (4 March 2022), https://hbr.org/2022/03/dont-underestimate-the-power-of-self-reflection, accessed 4 November 2024

39 Chouinard, Y, 'Earth is now our only shareholder', Patagonia (no date), https://

NOTES

eu.patagonia.com/gb/en/ownership/#, accessed 4 November 2024

40 Institute of Child Psychology, Episode 24, 'How to Nurture Executive Functioning in Teens with Dr. Ann-Louise Lockart' (2024), www.youtube.com/watch?v=LWzJfdaBHsQ, accessed 4 November 2024

41 Openexo, 'Abundance Mindset' (no date), https://openexo.com/book/1705-abundance-mindset, accessed 4 November 2024

42 Greatness Authors, 'Sadhguru's Wisdom: What the Mind of a Yogi & Visionary Has to Teach Us About Our Purpose', Greatness (18 July 2023), https://greatness.com/sadhguru-wisdom-mind-of-a-yogi-and-visionary, accessed 4 November 2024

43 Stanford, 'Steve Jobs' 2005 Stanford Commencement Address' (2008), www.youtube.com/watch?v=UF8uR6Z6KLc, accessed 4 November 2024

44 United Nations, 'Sustainable Development Goals' (no date), www.un.org/sustainabledevelopment/sustainable-development-goals, accessed 4 November 2024

45 Kurzweil, R, 'Understanding the Accelerating Rate of Change', the Kurzweil Library + collections (2 May 2003), www.thekurzweillibrary.com/understanding-the-accelerating-rate-of-change, accessed 4 November 2024

46 World Economic Forum, 'The Global Risks Report 2024, 19th Edition' (2024), www3.weforum.org/docs/WEF_The_Global_Risks_Report_2024.pdf, accessed 12 October 2024

47 Royal Shakespeare Company, 'Famous Quotes' (no date), www.rsc.org.uk/hamlet/about-the-play/famous-quotes, accessed 4 November 2024

Further Reading

Alzheimer's Association, *Art and Music* (no date), www.alz.org/help-support/caregiving/daily-care/art-music, accessed 12 October 2024

Anthony, M, Creative Development in Adolescents (Scholastic Parents, no date), www.scholastic.com/parents/family-life/creativity-and-critical-thinking/development-milestones/creative-development-adolescents.html, accessed 12 October 2024

Bergman, E, 'Autism and dance: does dancing benefit autistic kids?', *Autism Parenting Magazine* (9 October 2024), www.autismparentingmagazine.com/dance-movement-benefits/, accessed 12 October 2024

Better Help, *Seven Tips to Overcome Stage Fright* (2024), www.betterhelp.com/advice/stage-fright/13-

tips-to-overcome-stage-fright/, accessed 12 October 2024

Child Mind Institute, *12 Tips for Raising Confident Kids* (2024), https://childmind.org/article/12-tips-raising-confident-kids/, accessed 12 October 2024

Fisher, J, 'Make it maverick: rethinking the "Make It Macho" strategy for men in ballet', *Dance Chronicle*, 30/1 (2007), 45–66, https://doi.org/10.1080/01472520601163854

Keiffer, R, 'Viewing dance as instinct with Professor Janet Lilly', *The Carolinian* (31 August 2016), https://carolinianuncg.com/2016/08/31/viewing-dance-as-instinct-with-professor-janet-lilly/, accessed 12 October 2024

Lakes, KD, Marvin, S Rowley, J, et al, 'Dancer perceptions of the cognitive, social, emotional, and physical benefits of modern styles of partnered dancing', *Complementary Therapies in Medicine*, 26 (2016), 117–122, www.sciencedirect.com/science/article/abs/pii/S0965229916300322, accessed 21 November 2024

Marks, H, *Stage Fright (Performance Anxiety)* (WebMD, 2024), www.webmd.com/anxiety-panic/stage-fright-performance-anxiety, accessed 12 October 2024

Michiels, C, 'Niveau van leerlingen in Vlaanderen daalde nog nooit zo snel', *VRT News* (5 December 2023), www.vrt.be/vrtnws/nl/2023/12/05/

FURTHER READING

onderwijs-pisa-resultaten-wiskunde-lezen-wetenschappen/, accessed 12 October 2024

Miriyam, M, *When World Athletes Did Ballet* (The Lewis Foundation of Classical Ballet, 2016), www.thelewisfoundation.org/2016/08/when-world-athletes-did-ballet/, accessed 12 October 2024

Oaklander, M, 'Bad posture makes you sad and afraid, study finds', Time (18 September 2014), https://time.com/3394589/slumping-makes-you-sad/, accessed 12 October 2024

Reynoldsburg City Schools, *The Benefits of Dance* (no date), www.reyn.org/Downloads/The_Benefits_of_Dance.pdf, accessed 12 October 2024

Ricci, T, 'For first time in history of Canada's National Ballet School, more boys than girls will graduate', *CBC* (19 September 2019), www.cbc.ca/news/canada/toronto/canadas-national-ballet-schools-graduating-class-1.5288565, accessed 12 October 2024

Saline, S, *Prioritize It! Teaching kids the difference between NOW and LATER* (no date), https://drsharonsaline.com/2020/02/17/prioritize-it-teaching-kids-the-difference-between-now-and-later/, accessed 12 October 2024

The Promenade Dance Studio, *Dance For Positive Social Interaction: Dancing with friends is good for your health* (no date), www.mddancesport.com/social-benefits-of-dance, accessed 12 October 2024

University of Sydney, *Dance Your Way to a Healthy Heart* (2016), www.sydney.edu.au/news-opinion/news/2016/03/02/dance-your-way-to-a-healthy-heart.html, accessed 12 October 2024

Vandevyvere, I, 'Big changes are on the horizon...', LinkedIn (2024), www.linkedin.com/posts/ineke-vandevyvere-60a4b6267_big-changes-are-on-the-horizon-in-my-life-activity-7143205043872157696-tvXH?utm_source=share&utm_medium=member_desktop, accessed 4 November 2024

World Health Organization, *Mental Health* (2022), www.who.int/news-room/fact-sheets/detail/mental-health-strengthening-our-response, accessed 12 October 2024

World Vision, *8 Ways to Raise World-Changing Kids* (2021), www.wvi.org/stories/child-sponsorship/8-ways-raise-world-changing-kids, accessed 12 October 2024

Acknowledgements

The creation of *The Dance Advantage* has been supported by numerous individuals whose contributions have been invaluable. We would like to extend our sincere gratitude to everyone mentioned here.

The dancers and their parents at Ndigo, whose participation and performances have given meaning to our work. Many dancers have continued dancing since they were four, and today, as young adults, we're blown away by how far you've come. As we often say, without you, our role as pedagogues would have no meaning.

We thank the BOSS remote team for their tireless efforts. They serve as our pillars of support, consistently contributing behind the scenes. Special recognition goes to Earl Dacal, our talented graphic designer, whose illustrations are sprinkled throughout this book.

To our Teacher Team, we thank you for your dedication and pursuit in raising the next generation of dancers. Some of you were once the young dancers standing in our classes as children. We thank you for your tireless work in creating classes, choreographies and much more.

The dance pedagogues who have mentored us, working patiently with us. Your guidance exemplifies the truth that behind every successful dancer is a mentor who believes in them.

Big thanks to all the schoolteachers for giving us the opportunity to interview you. A special thank you to the dance parents for sharing your experiences through interviews and testimonials. Your personal stories have enriched this book immensely.

We are particularly indebted to dance professionals Jee-Eun Petitqueux, Stephan Vodenitcharov, Pedro Szalay and Sander Blommaert for their support, patience as test readers, participation in numerous Zoom calls and interviews, and their stellar contributions to the dance world. Your views and beliefs have made their way into this book and have been crucial to the development of our ideas.

ACKNOWLEDGEMENTS

Finally, we wouldn't have come so far without our families, especially our parents, Johan, Leen, James and Angela, and we thank them for their unwavering support of our endeavours, both in helping raise Milan and in our decisions regarding Ndigo. Your belief in us has always been the foundation of our success.

We thank you, our readers, whose interest in this book makes you part of our journey to raise creative and resilient children for tomorrow.

Once again, a huge thanks to the collective efforts of all those involved that have made *The Dance Advantage* a reality. We hope it will serve as a valuable resource in the nurturing of young dancers and individuals for years to come.

The Authors

Our story is one of love, partnership and, of course, dance. We started on different continents but ended up at the Fontys Dansacademie in Tilburg, The Netherlands. Justin was born in India and studied choreography; Ineke was born in Belgium and studied dance pedagogy. Our love for dance was the foundation for both a personal and professional partnership.

In 2009, we took the leap and founded Ndigo, our dance and yoga studio. This was the start of our entrepreneurial journey in the dance world, a journey that has touched the lives of tens of thousands of people and their families over more than fifteen years. Our students have gone on to study at The Royal Ballet London, L'Opera Paris, Royal Ballet Antwerp, Fontys Dansacademie and de! Kunsthumaniora Contemporary Dance Antwerp...

We love to learn, so we went to New York to study at the American Ballet Theater NTC's teacher degree. After the course, we were inspired and re-energised by the experience and the mentors we met. We incorporated the new insights we'd gained into our teaching at Ndigo and we were rewarded for our hard work. Here are a few:

- Best Artistic Director award in 2023
- Nine-time Belgian Champions for Contemporary and ballet
- Two-time European Champions for Contemporary and ballet
- Best Dance Pedagogues in 2024
- Junior Grand Prix at the New Prague Dance Festival in 2024

As husband and wife, parents and business partners, we navigate life's ups and downs together. Our partnership goes beyond the studio as we run a dance school and raise a family.

What drives us is our deep desire to make an impact.

We believe in the power of dance to transform lives, not just locally but globally. We are proud to support children with Plan International, like Awtesh in India and Genesis Ayala in El Salvador. For fifteen years, we helped Awtesh go to school and saw how education can make someone's life better. When that chapter ended, we jumped at the chance to help Genesis.

We've also partnered with B1G1, linking our business activities directly to global charitable causes. For instance, when a child is enrolled in one of our camps, we provide five days of clean drinking water to a school in Zambia. Other initiatives include meals, multivitamins and art classes for young children.

Ndigo also supports rural communities. We learned that even a few hundred euros can go a long way in building a vocational school in rural India to empower women. A woman can learn to sew, earn extra income, and keep her children in school. Those are life-changing actions.

Even though it's not as big as building spaceships that can travel to other planets, we think these small changes can make a big difference.

Through Ndigo, and now this book, we want to share our love for dance and inspire innovation and courage in the next generation of dancers. We are excited to share our experiences and knowledge through *The Dance Advantage*. It's not just our professional knowledge, but our personal journey and love for nurturing young talent. We hope that, through this book, we can reach more people and inspire creativity and resilience in children and adults beyond the walls of our studio.

Follow us:

- www.ndigo.be
- www.linkedin.com/in/inekevandevyvere
- www.linkedin.com/in/justinyep
- www.instagram.com/ndigoroeselare
- www.youtube.com/@ndigoroeselare
- www.facebook.com/Ndigoroeselare

www.ingramcontent.com/pod-product-compliance
Lightning Source LLC
Chambersburg PA
CBHW010429190426
43201CB00047BA/2335